We all deeply yearn to be heard, listened to, and understood, to be free from the loneliness of our own experiences, and instead, bring someone else along the ride, someone who can become our reflection, our mirror, that holds our secrets, our devilishness, and our divinity, however, we seldom allow ourselves to listen, listen to the sound, to the ambiance, and to the listener, to the one that transformed himself into the vessel that holds the secrets to all that is. This work is a sum up of what the listener has to say.

To my father, the one who was my critic, my friend, and most importantly, my teacher, without you this work wouldn't have come to life. I thank you with a heart full of gratitude and appreciation. And to my cat, Bunny, who was my companion along writing every single page of this book, you made this ride far more beautiful.

Rand Emad

HOW TO CONQUER YOUR NEGATIVE EMOTIONS

AUSTIN MACAULEY PUBLISHERS™

LONDON • CAMBRIDGE • NEW YORK • SHARJAH

A CIP catalogue record for this title is available from the British Library.

ISBN 9781035827725 (Paperback)
ISBN 9781035827732 (ePub e-book)

www.austinmacauley.com

First Published 2024
Austin Macauley Publishers Ltd®
1 Canada Square
Canary Wharf
London
E14 5AA

Table of Contents

Preface

The very first breath you breathe symbolises the magnificent entrance of your soul to this life; with the highest purity of body, mind, and soul, you enter the starting point for a long trip that holds within it folds many twists and turns, lessons, and aspirations that call your name to accomplish.

Life gradually begins to shape its meaning as you slowly develop your sense of self, this formation occurs through different attempts to create an identity that provides you with power, happiness, and security in the hope of living a life of meaning and joy, however, what you do not realise is that with these newly developed self-identifications comes a price, that price is you creating your restrictions, where you unconsciously draw the illusion of personal freedom, and consequently end up demolishing the free spirit of the child within you, leading a life of repression and misery. your self-imposed restrictions will be like a haunting ghost staring at you through the night.

It is a liberating realisation to learn that you may be your own worst enemy, that you have all the keys to achieving inner harmony and balance as a human being, and that you can make the conscious decision to face whatever it is that scares you, and most importantly, to face your dark side, and to understand that the strong desire to escape yourself is a sign that you need to address and heal your wounds to live a happy and blissful life.

You must be willing to embark on a long journey that involves much searching, dissecting, and sometimes even deconstructing many aspects of who you are, such as your cherished beliefs, your sense of self, and your habits, all for the purified version of your soul to emerge, that is if you want to create a better understanding of yourself.

Most of our suffering results from psychological or emotional traumas caused by others with whom we share experiences or by unavoidable unpleasant life events. While the causes of our suffering may vary, the outcomes remain consistent: a destructive emotional nature that thrives on destroying itself and others, manifesting itself in the form of emotions that were formed early in life and gradually unleashing themselves to manifest ruin and catastrophes. The odd thing is that we frequently succumb to this destructive power, believing that ignoring its obvious truth will somehow address the situation, but in reality, what occurs is that we wind up trudging through life with a victim mentality rather than taking full responsibility for who we are and the limited time we have on this earth.

The central point that must be understood and internalised is that your emotions create your deepest motives, which are at the root of every action, reaction, and sometimes even self-destruction and that in order to live a conscious life, you must dig deep within yourself and cultivate the endurance to accept your emotional and psychological state. Furthermore, to recognise that self-denial in all of its forms is the pitfall that many people fall into throughout their lives. Being unable to identify who you are as a human, your purpose, your emotions, your likes and dislikes, and your boundaries is the source of your misery; such denial will not only destroy your inner being but will also affect your relationships, causing them to fail, because you are a person who denies their true self and their needs.

It's essential to prepare yourself to be vulnerable and to open your eyes to all that is not so beautiful about you. You must develop a pure and unbiased vision that resembles a mirror that reflects every part of who you are in the light of truth.

This way, you can see yourself for who you are. While this process may be painful, because it will shatter every illusion you've internalised within yourself, you shall remain receptive and enthusiastic because this is the starting point for self-development, the development that will translate itself onto your surroundings, relationships, and everything you touch.

This book discusses human emotions, their causes and effects, and how they may be converted into a new level of self-empowerment, a shift in perception, and, ultimately, a change in reality.

May you reach your greatest potential.

Fear

Fear has been deep-rooted in the human psyche throughout centuries of man's search for survival; it was an ingrained defence system that helped humans survive through the most primitive ways of existing; however, in this day and age, fear has taken on a different form, one that is more psychological, and centred around social acceptance or rejection; it has also become far more subtle and invisible, and even frowned upon and viewed as a sign of fragility when expressed, and while it has taken on a more reserved form, it is still very much alive and ravaging the way we experience life, where we end up living on the borderline of whether we should get involved or hold back, should we take off or delay our desire to pursue, it's a dilemma that we all suffer from, the questions that come to mind are, how can we handle our fear? Does self-preservation require a certain level of self-restraint? And is liberation from fear nothing but a mere illusion?

All of these different questions, in essence, lead to the same goal: how can we better understand ourselves? How can we raise our awareness of our fears? And most importantly, how can we overcome the restrictions that we've inherited?

First, we must define fear as a robust emotional response to a perceived physical or psychological threat. Its potent effects manifest as physical symptoms such as excessive sweating, trembling, and even difficulty breathing. The central point is that fear is the first line of defence of human emotions because it signifies the most difficult challenge a person will face in life. Because it is tied to mental fear, it may sometimes become a type of weakness when it is intertwined with one's psychological wants and desires, in such cases, emotions of fear don't require physical stimulants, but rather one's awareness of his surrounding ends up generating it. It becomes, in a sense, an ongoing inner epic that repeats itself in response to even little stimuli.

To distinguish between required innate fear and fear based on knowledge and experience, which is what we experience today, we must return to a time when a human lived a primordial existence based on natural foundations. During that time, since there was no verbal communication between people and no manual for nature's perils, a human had to rely on his innate survival skills. In turn, the senses produced emotional stimulants that would alert him to impending danger.

This created a state of extreme alertness that made humans receptive to hazards, which kept them awake and focused on ensuring that they survived. In today's world, with the development of language and knowledge, we may appear to have become far less primitive and more civil, but in our essence, we still have the remnants of that same primal man who was fighting to survive, today; we are highly watchful of others and their opinions about us, we are cautious about our actions only because they may be frowned upon by others, the issue here is that we are governed by fear, not by awareness.

This dilemma could be blamed on our societal policies that use fear to instil order and structure in the masses, as fear is an emotion that can be easily aroused and is potent enough to tame and control any faulty behaviour. While this type of programming serves the purpose of creating a system, it's side effects generally go unnoticed and only reveal themselves in how frigid and dull we experience life. The question that arises is, how can we fight such a semblance of mental programming and regain our emotional freedom? The answer is simple yet complicated in its folds, and it is that we need to wake up from our mental idleness and instead work on our self-awareness because consciousness is what will allow us to function from a place of clarity instead of drowning in ignorance, it is what will enable us to take charge of our lives and free ourselves from fear. Isn't this the ultimate freedom, to be able to walk through life fearlessly?

You must go deep within yourself since here is where the process starts in order to discover the inner causes of your fear and its outward manifestations. This realisation will be the first step towards letting go of unconscious compulsions and gradually bringing to the surface what needs to be addressed and healed.

Causation

Threat

A threat is a statement of intent to inflict pain, injury, damage, or other hostile action on another person, and it can be inflicted physically, psychologically, or emotionally.

When you hear the word threat, will your reaction be to envision the risks you will encounter, or will you feel the danger that always surrounds you due to hearing threat, and does this cause you to fear confrontations? And what about the psychological and emotional threat? Are you aware of this type of danger and its consequences? Furthermore, have you ever considered why you tend to avoid critical confrontations or why you stay attached to situations or people who intentionally hurt you? These questions may appear unrelated, but as we describe this notion, you will be able to connect the dots and discover that you have spent much of your life feeling threatened and terrified.

First, to fully comprehend this intangible form of danger, we must understand what an identity is. Identity is one's sense of self that one shapes through experiences, relationships, and knowledge; these three aspects play a primary role in moulding one's character and determining its expressions in this world; this understanding will help us to accept the fact that our identities are what govern our existence and shape the course of our lives; as a result, we spend a significant amount of effort maintaining our identities.

The need for protection is frequently transformed into feelings of fear and nervousness because the perceived danger threatens our circle in which we find emotional security and safety, the (I), a part of our existence that we cannot jeopardise, so we react by declaring war on the threatening person. We arm ourselves with means of protection preparing to attack at any given moment. The issue here is that this reaction stems from an unconscious need for protection that does not find actual realisation, but instead governs one's emotions and behaviour without his awareness; this is a sign of a lack of self-awareness because individuals who cultivate a deep understanding of their inner self can regulate their emotions and control their reactions, as opposed to those who don't understand their internal map and, as a result, they crash in the face of danger.

Another factor that contributes to the arousal of such feelings is the solid emotional investment we have in our beliefs and ideas, as these are the foundations of our personalities. As a result, we take opposition personally, resulting in quarrels and disagreements between individuals. It is a mind game of survival that relies on self-protection mechanisms that stem from fear, where we must prove and establish our beliefs; otherwise, what if the other person presents a more credible argument? What if he formulates a more logical point? We all have this dread that someone else's beliefs would demolish ours; if so, who would we be, and what is our identity now? In some way, it's a real threat of losing ourselves.

This type of threat centres around mental prospects, which is why conversations involving opposing opinions about a belief system or strong ideas tend to go in terrible directions because both parties are emotionally invested in their beliefs and will try to protect them at all costs, even if it means sabotaging the other person or attempting to invalidate them. It is fear driving this tactic and evoking the need to get out of the argument as a whole. When, in actuality, this conflict is nothing more than a figment of the imagination.

A threat can also take a purely emotional form, where its implications are precisely directed towards one's emotions. We see many people using this dynamic tactic of instilling fear in others to manipulate and control, in an attempt to dictate their relationships and gain authority. This manipulation can manifest in many different ways and have various effects, but it is primarily based on the central point of power and control, and that is, the more terrified a person is, the weaker they are, and as a consequence, one may gain more power and influence over events and others.

For example, in a fear-based relationship, one person intimidates the other to get what they want, preying on the other's insecurities and flaws to gain control and gradually break him down. The implied threats can take the form of words, actions, or even subliminal messages, and they are often effective in inducing fear because such manipulative individuals instinctively know their perfect victim; they are the ones that have a natural inclination to panic and dread, and who are quickly shook and terrified. The response of such people tends to go in one of two directions: one, they fall and surrender all their power in the hopes of not losing a part with which they associate their sense of security, or two, they become highly rash and aggressive with their behaviour. These are two different reactions, but they are conjoined with the fact that such people are rarely able to break the vicious cycle of abuse due to how controlled they are by their fear and insecurity.

It is critical to pay attention to your relationship dynamics and understand other people's motives, intentions, and the patterns that shape their behaviour towards you because these aspects will reveal to you what you need to know about the nature of your connections and whether they contribute to your happiness or misery.

The original creators of this tactic, authority figures, always use emotional and psychological threats to establish and maintain their power. This omnipresent strategy built the world we live in today, and while its methods change, its uses and effectiveness remain potent. On a more personal level, you must have sensed that authority figures in your life try to control you, your ideas and ways of thinking, and every minor decision you make. Their goal is to create an obedient character who can be easily manipulated and controlled, like a puppet, so that they can maintain their power. This strategy is linked to many people's ignorance about leadership and guidance, so when they find themselves in a position of power, they fall back on the methods of discipline that they were taught, and as a result, they end up raising generations of conformists who follow the crowds and lack awareness. But, how can one tell the difference between a noble authority figure and one who is only interested in expanding his power? The answer is that a true mentor will tailor his advice and teachings to your personality, goals, and aspirations; by supporting and refining your vision, he will pave the way for you to find your independent lane and not attempt to deflect his desires on you; once you understand the difference, you will be able to distinguish a true mentor from a fake one.

Lastly, certain people may feel threatened by anything threatening their fictitious vision of reality. Such people misinterpret the world around them to protect themselves from psychological and emotional suffering. By forming alternate versions of reality and remaining in a state of illusion, they achieve a temporary sense of emotional security. They create a protective mental and emotional barrier between them and what might cause them to suffer, this may appear to be a form of self-protection, but it is a dangerous self-deception that can lead to more misfortunes and catastrophes because refusing to acknowledge a problem does not make it magically disappear; instead, it remains to lurk beneath the surface until it multiplexes and expands enough to explode, and that point is one you don't want to reach because it is the point of utmost destruction and disaster. However, reaching the point of disillusionment is a complex challenge because once the disrupted perception of reality is established, it is mentally rationalised and emotionally supported, resulting in a chain of mental and emotional connection that is difficult to break and makes confronting a part of the brutal reality difficult. Another group of people who fall into the same trap are those who never developed a clear insight that views reality in its entirety; they were overprotected as children and weren't allowed to go through experiences and discover their environment; as a result, they grow up with a significant lack in their realisation of the dangers that world holds, believing that naivety is a virtue and that hiding out the unpleasant aspects of life is the antidote for misery, they discard an inseparable part of reality, which ends casting a pall over their reality, and since they resort to deceiving themselves to protect and maintain the illusionary structure of their existence from being destroyed and dismantled, they remain in a bubble that can easily be burst, but this leaves them in a constant state of defence against anything that threatens to shatter their delusion, where they fight an internal battle of fear and anxiety, but when they come face to face with something powerful enough to destroy their phantasm and expose them to the light of truth, they suffer horribly because they never allowed themselves to experience pain and learn from it.

Remember that a lesson postponed is a lesson multiplied!

Death

Have you ever considered that the only certain thing in life on this planet is that it will end and that no matter how different our lives are, we are all united by one thing: death? This truth is fascinating, frightening, and paradoxical all at once because what divides us is ultimately what brings us all together.

Knowing that each and every life will end one day is extremely powerful. The ending is what gives life its significance and purpose. Imagine If you were eternal. Will your life have any meaning? Your limited time in this life is what gives you a strong sense of the value of your time and how to live life to its fullest potential; it is one beautiful road trip that you're taking and loving every minute of it, an inevitable fate that you must go through, to live every day as if it's your last with acceptance of what is unavoidable, and even though death is the only certainty in our lives, many people avoid thinking about it and regard it as something hidden or from the underworld, even though it is something we will all confront at some point in our lives and experience via the death of loved ones.

Many of us view death as a mystical experience, and some view it as an inescapable fateful experience. We form this opinion based on our fear of the unknown and our sense of connection to this world because it is the only thing we have ever known. Try to imagine that all the life in you will slowly leave your body, you will take your last breath, and that this will be the most singular experience you will ever have; it's incredible. The moment your life ends, you will discover how you have mistaken your existence for loneliness and that every time you got crazy because you were on your own, it was simply that you were running away from yourself. Imagine if you were flying and looking from above at your soul as it left your body; fully knowing that it is the moment of departure; at that exact moment, you will appreciate the uniqueness of your life, and for the first time, you will understand the nature of your existence and reconcile with it.

Remember that most of us are ruled by our fear of death in various hidden and unconscious ways, unaware that how we view and comprehend death will hugely impact how we approach life.

Realise the truth: The people who are uptight and rigid in their approach to life are the ones who have yet to recognise their mortal nature; they take life too seriously and race to exceed the societal standard for success; being too caught up in this race, they forget to create their concept of happiness, and end up living to please their environment and society. Their limited understanding of reality and fear of falling behind in their imagined race of life causes them to focus their energies on gaining tangible benefits and improving their social position while fearing to explore other aspects of life and comprehend their mortality. When the unavoidable occurs, they are struck by the painful reality of death. They are usually the ones who suffer the most and undergo a complete perceptional transformation by the force of circumstances, where they receive a wake-up call that awakens them to the essence of life and existence, which is a key and powerful occurrence in life since it is the time when one's attention is focused to the essential features of life, allowing him to put everything into proper perspective.

Sufferers: The other group of people is those who have thought about death or even experienced the loss of a loved one, and as a result, they've had to recognise death. This shock has only increased their fear of death and attachment to life to the point where they adopt a careless attitude that centres their existence around pleasure. The problem with this attitude is that it's a form of escapism caused by fear, in which one diverts his attention away from life's hard and painful truths by engaging in any pleasure-inducing activity. However, because pleasure is fleeting and can only last so long, this attitude breeds dependency and weakness in one's character, as one here fluctuates between an extreme high and a deep low, which is in no way a healthy way of living because he becomes unable to work effectively or cope with pain without a distracting pleasure.

You must realise that the fear of death causes an impediment in one's experience of life; it generates a feeling of distortion to reality, where one cannot cope with the essence of his existence, so he seeks methods to distract himself from the anguish involved with facing and accepting this fact.

When we look closely at how we spend our lives, we will find that what we all do is an escape from our mortal nature, unaware that our flight is but a new experience of failure that we will carry forward.

The law: Accepting reality is the first step towards actually living it; denying or escaping any truth in life will keep you imprisoned, and when we're talking about such a truth as death, it is critical to accept it as a significant part of reality in order to live a dignified fulfilling life that respects the true meaning of existence. Keeping this truth in mind will liberate you from many fears you may experience and serve as your disciplinarian because only when you consider your life's ending will you be able to put things into perspective and give everything its actual value.

The Imagination

The human mind is a profound enigma because of its power to reshape the world and attain the highest heights of grandeur and invention; consider what the human mind has generated; many bright minds have been able to improve humanity's living conditions, allowing us to live in a more pleasant and comfortable environment. However, the mind's enormous power was only made possible by the faculty of imagination, which is the ability to create a mental image of something that is not apparent to the senses. This remarkable capacity is one of our greatest assets as humans; however, it has turned into a mental prison for people who use it to produce visions of catastrophe, sorrow, and disaster.

We spend a significant amount of our lives pondering a wide range of ideas, circumstances, and events; this is a natural part of human nature and aids in developing new ideas, prediction, and problem-solving. The path along which your mind conducts these contemplations is primarily dictated by your prior experiences and general temperament, where you view the world and form your thoughts based on what you have experienced earlier in life; a positive individual, for example, will use this faculty to imagine desired outcomes, whereas a negative individual or one in a negative mental state will navigate his thoughts to imagine unwanted outcomes and suffering, and despite the lack of existential existence or proof, these thoughts still elicit emotional responses of fear and anxiety, because mental imagery is so powerful and effective in producing emotional and mental reactions, most individuals are unaware of this. As a result, they fall into the trap of utilising their imagination to predict their anxiety and sadness before they occur, resulting in a disturbed emotional state that hinders them from going on and following their objectives and desires.

Consider it a key that starts with a single thought. For example, if you are contemplating starting a new project and have had a pleasant and positive life experience thus far, you will consider the completion and success of your project.

In contrast, if you have had unfortunate incidents, you will visualise all the failures and obstacles that you will face in attempting to create this project; in the latter situation, your mind follows patterns of fear, anxiety, and misfortune, and your thoughts induce more and more of the same emotional state, the crux of the matter is that you are using your imagination to amplify your pre-existing fear and despair by visualising images of what is unfavourable, don't send to your unconscious mind negative images.

What you need to understand is that your mind follows patterns of what it knows and what it can predict, so you generally imagine things similar to what you have already experienced, whether positive or negative. However, mental imagery has no existential existence in either case, so you must recognise this fact and detach yourself from any negative images that may appear in your mind; furthermore, to interrupt the cycle of negativity and train your mind to think

30

positively. You must learn to detect when your mind begins to wander in a negative path because if you can capture this moment instantaneously, you will be able to redirect your thoughts into a more positive route, and over time modify the patterns of your thinking, your mind is like a wild horse, hold its rein.

Shoot the arrow: It is essential to realise that you are the one who generates the idea, and as the generator, you have the power to destroy it as well. When you come to this realisation, you will stop paying attention to all the negative imagery in your head, and you will develop a sense of detachment from what is happening inside your mind. And while some of us are more imaginative than others, it is a capacity that we all possess and can positively develop in various ways. It is critical to use this tremendous power of the mind to its maximum potential and to achieve everything you put your mind to; using your imagination and aiding it with the proper action will help you come up with wonderful ideas and know how you want your future to be. Using your imagination and assisting it with the appropriate action can help you achieve everything you desire in life.

Rejection

You are wonderful: Have you ever thought about how much it means to be liked and respected by others around you? And why is the prospect of being rejected so terrible and devastating to you? Essentially, we all have an enormous urge to love and be loved; but we seldom go deep within ourselves to discover the genuine source of this desire, and as a result, we become so entangled with its complexity that it becomes a cause of dread and anguish rather than a driving force for life.

Rejection in any form, whether interpersonal, emotional, or social, can significantly impact our self-esteem, well-being, and overall quality of life. It is devastating to be rejected by society, family, or a romantic partner because such occurrences are commonly interpreted as a sign of not being good enough or worthy of love, and this sensation is both excruciating and harmful.

We've all experienced rejection and reacted to it uniquely; remember that morning when you said hello to that stranger and got a side eye, when you were so in love with someone who rejected you completely, or when your family rejected your lifestyle or personality. I remind you that we've all dealt with this feeling, whether briefly or more profoundly, though in essence, the meaning we assign to rejection is a significant factor in determining its impact; for example, if a rejection incident meant to you that you are unlovable, foolish, or unattractive, you are more likely to be profoundly impacted and emotionally upset by it, because you have assigned the meaning that this rejection means I'm unworthy of love, In this case, your thought process, in which you attributed your worth to an external source, elicited even more unpleasant feelings than usual.

The key: Fear manifests itself more strongly in the aftermath of rejection, and it is here that most individuals become trapped. Because the first experience of being rejected aroused some profoundly unpleasant and painful feelings, to the point where one gets increasingly terrified of having this experience replicated ever again, and therefore the fear becomes a significantly more long-term fight to overcome.

For most of us, this struggle is unfulfilled and unconscious because it manifests itself not through true feelings of fear but rather through a state of immobility that prevents us from taking productive action; this immobility stems not from the inability to move nor from the rejection itself, but rather from the fear of experiencing the same pain again.

Know your problem: Think about it; you will find that the desire to not repeat painful experiences is valid; however, when this desire becomes incapacitating and a cause of passivity, it becomes a problem that must be addressed; otherwise, you will find yourself on the verge of wanting to progress but unable to overcome your ingrained fear of suffering.

Open the door: Now the question is, how can you understand and distinguish your fear in order to overcome it? First, you must recognise that whenever you have an urge to pursue something while feeling unable to act on that desire, fear is definitely involved, and often this fear is centred around not being accepted, in other words, rejected.

Know yourself: Try to inspect this feeling; what are you trying to avoid, pain, suffering, humiliation? But first and foremost, why do you believe that not being accepted by someone is terrible? On this subject, you must pause and reflect because when you go deeper within yourself to find answers to this question, you will notice two important aspects: one, how do you view yourself, do you have confidence in your abilities? And two, what do other's opinions represent for you, are they other perspectives that are fun to explore and understand, or are they a foundation on which you build yourself? When you locate the answers, you will see that your fear of rejection arises from a lack of self-confidence; you are not empowered by your identity but instead rely on others to empower you through it.

Don't play the victim: This attitude of viewing others as a means to validate your inner self will not only cause you much internal struggle but will also weaken your spirit and inner power because this stance is all about hunger for something you can't provide for yourself, which signifies an underlying internal lack of self-assurance and emotional fulfilment.

The interesting thing is that we often think of rejection as fear of deprivation of love and validation, when, in truth, it's more about looking for an external source of what we're missing emotionally, these two suggestions may appear to be identical, but they express two opposing perspectives: one is about dependency and using others as emotional stimulants, while the other is about responsibility and accountability for one's inner self, the latter may appear to be ruthless and insensitive to emotional needs, but do you prefer to be a victim of life and others or the driving force behind your life?

Confidence: We cannot deny the significance and importance of being accepted by others, not only emotionally and psychologically, but also in increasing our chances of achieving our goals and aspirations; however, this desire should not become a source of fear; you must understand that today's world, unlike the past, has grown to be far more diverse and inclusive than ever before; now, more than ever. You have the opportunity to discover like-minded individuals who share your beliefs and aspirations, and you have several avenues to express yourself; being rejected by an individual or social group no longer represents a loss in your odds of survival, but rather a denial of an emotional need; nonetheless, this need must be examined and understood to free yourself from your unconscious impulses that drive your needs and the fear centred around them.

The Unknown

What is knowledge: It is awareness of a set of experiences gained from living an actual reality; this awareness can only happen through the senses and the mind's capacity to evaluate observations. Our knowledge is essentially the lens through which we see the world, and it creates and highlights the form of who we are based on our reactions and decisions to the external world.

Release your fear: We consider knowledge to be a significant source of power and intelligence because valuable information on any given subject can lead us to desired outcomes and envisioned goals; however, if this is the case, why do we frequently experience fear and anxiety about our life path and direction? If knowledge is the source of power, why are we constantly terrified of the future, life mysteries, and others? Is it because we are too rigid and committed to what we already know that we lose our ability to adapt to new and unexpected knowledge, facts, and truths? Or because self-preservation automatically necessitates vigilance and attentiveness to the unfamiliar and unexplored that it is natural to experience emotions of fear, both suggestions have merit, but what we truly need is to find ways to be open to life and liberate ourselves from the fear formed around the unknown, because only by doing so will we be able to broaden our horizons and explore the true nature of our existence.

Your driving force: We try to find comfort by organising our minds and attaching ourselves to sets of ideas, beliefs, and morals; we find relief and assurance in knowing that we can categorise, dissect, and distinguish between what is desired and what is undesired because it is only through this ability that we can bring more of what we want and eliminate what causes us pain and suffering. It is our inner circle that we turn to in the face of any challenging situation; however, when this circle is faced with new or foreign information and conditions, we find that most of us become filled with panic and fear due to the feelings of not being equipped or ready to handle such adversity. When we dig deeper to try and find the root causes for this fear, we discover that it is because we operate in our lives by accumulating enough information and understanding repeated patterns rather than from pure awareness of the moment.

Up to a certain point in our lives, we stop utilising our senses in order to fully understand the moment but rather depend on our previously gathered knowledge to make judgments. The problem is that we unknowingly cease being receptive to new knowledge because of how strongly we are tied to what we already know, and as a result, we lose the youthful spirit that dwells in our being, which wants to explore and is open to the formless nature of life.

Don't hesitate: For every one of us, the fear of the unknown manifests itself in many ways, ranging from the fear of mortality, which is the source of all fears, to the fear of the future, which we all suffer. The need to control every detail of our lives and the outcomes of situations is so strong that the prospect of a mysterious tomorrow is terrifying; this need for control stems from an inability to cope with not knowing; our day-to-day lives require us to calculate and analyse various situations in order to achieve desired outcomes and solve problems; we become so engrossed in this mental process and its calculations that we lose sight of the bigger picture, and as a result, we become filled with fear and anxiety. Furthermore, we frequently fail to see that such a way of living stifles our potential to learn and grow our knowledge and awareness of the world.

Fly with your imagination: It is essential to have a set of ideas and beliefs that serve your growth and expansion, but it's just as important to not get too attached to any of them and to remain open and perceptive to the world around you; imagine your bias towards what you know as a wall that protects you from the outside world's cruelty and danger, and while it does serve its purpose of protecting you, it also imprisons you. You must acknowledge that there is a big universe beyond your comprehension and that a large part of your mission is to explore this enormous world and its magnificence. Cultivating the capacity to surrender yourself to life's possibilities will not only empower you but will also diminish most of your fears.

Outcomes

Aggressiveness

Your fears: Fear is a form of self-defence; it reacts to anything threatening our identity and what we hold dear and precious to us. And, despite the differences in our personal beliefs, our responses to threats to the values that construct our identities are often similar in nature; they are layers of self-protection built around the fear itself, the fear of loss, failure, judgment, and hurt, we innately wish to avoid suffering and protect our emotional safety and well-being; and many times, this unconscious urge, which derives from fear, frequently manifests as an aggressive and combative reaction to anything that could potentially bring pain or destruction to our identities.

Don't hide yourself: Fear often causes us to feel anxious, vulnerable, and in danger; these feelings are difficult to process and they drain much of our energy; and as a result of how dreadful these feelings are, we attempt to find methods through which we can cope and soothe down the discomfort associated with these feelings; the most prominent is aggression, consider aggression as your own reaction to your fear; a metaphorical armour that protects and disguises vulnerability in times of anxiousness and danger, for in such moments, it is inconvenient and dangerous to expose your inner weakness to the outside world and others, because they might exploit and use these emotions to manipulate and control you, and as a result, the innate need to feel safe guides you to resort to creating a protective layer that helps you feel more empowered and in command, and thus seem more robust and intimidating to others, and although this reaction might make you feel more capable in the face of a threat or apprehension, it does not address or assist you overcome your actual fears.

Your armour: The protection strategy initially begins with the sole need to protect the identity and what supports it. In this stage, an individual is generally consumed with finding ways to validate himself and not necessarily focused on the other, and the aggression here manifests in one's attitude of defensiveness and antipathy, if the level of fear heightens, an individual goes one step further by not only focusing on protecting himself, but also by trying to invalidate the other person's stance, emotions, or ideas. Here the urge to protect is more potent than the latter and tends to focus on both self-protection by establishing a position and belittling the other. In the final stage of aggression, the individual takes on the stance of the destroyer; he becomes solely focused on destroying and dismantling the other, losing all awareness and empathy, revealing the primal aspect of his core being, the animal urge to kill or be killed, where all rules are meaningless. The need to survive centres the fight around who gets to come out alive. This final stage is the most dangerous because its uncalculated results tend to lead to the utmost destruction and ruin.

Don't carry your fears: You must understand that your need for protection is essentially motivated by a wide range of your rooted worries, for they unconsciously create a sense of threat and alertness towards the outside world and its varying differences.

If you are constantly confronting opposition with aggression, you must realise that this reaction doesn't stem from power but an inner sense of shakiness and fear; it may seem convenient to resort to this way of reacting to the external world because it is part of your habitual patterns of behaviour and second nature, however, constantly reacting to your inner fear with aggression and projecting it onto the outside world will not only disallow you to cultivate better self-awareness but will also further deepen the roots of your fear.

Define your goal: Begin to investigate the reasons for your aggression, and try to spot the moment in which you shut your receptivity to others; this is a crucial moment to recognise because this is when the protection mode is on, and this point can guide you directly to one of your deep-rooted fears, developing the ability to investigate your inner self will gradually but steadily elevate your level of awareness and broaden your knowledge of who you are, and that will not only allow you to liberate yourself from all your fears but will also enable you to have better connections with others and handle conflicts and quarrels.

Stagnation

Contemplate: The essence of life is in its motion; even in the quietest atmospheres, movement occurs; consider how the sun lightens up the morning sky and shifts throughout the day to make room for the moon to appear and provide some light to the darkness of the night; this motion is what creates the life within this universe and the life that each of us has; every move you make in your life is what creates the next; your life is a constant state of moving towards or away from something.

Your emotions: Emotions, without a doubt, have a significant effect on the decisions and actions we make in our lives. They influence our perceptions of the world and; as a result, our actions. Fear is by far the most debilitating and constricting emotion of all, as it creates an inner sense of uncertainty and instability that prevents us from taking confident and assured actions. The internal uncertainty is primarily caused by the preoccupation with self-protection and defence, as well as the attempt to predict outcomes; the engrossment in these various aspects blocks our ability to decide on and carry out an action, leaving us stuck in an inner battle that is difficult to overcome.

Fear is without a doubt one of the most powerful emotions; it's coded in the human psyche that yearns for continuity and survival, but when this urge transports from existential needs into psychological ones, a problem arises because a person filled with fear is stuck within the shackles of his mental world and its battles instead of being focused on reality and variants. If this state persists, one will eventually become stagnant and unmoving because his willpower and capacity to overcome barriers are weakened and undermined by fear, to the point where the primary substance of his existence is to live in a continual state of motion, is blocked.

The trash bin: The condition of stagnation might be caused by an external obstacle. We cannot deny that life can occasionally throw roadblocks and challenges in our way, preventing us from accomplishing our objectives and desires; but, often enough, our standstill is typically caused by internal fixation with fear. Consider why some people seem to be able to navigate through life's troubles while others become trapped; why some people always have solutions to issues while others always drown in them. Of course, various factors influence an individual's ability to overcome obstacles, such as life experience, mental strength, and executive skills, but the one that is most important and often underappreciated is emotional strength and the ability to deal with emotions of fear. In contrast to the person who is continuously obsessed with dread and worry and, as a result, is unable to confront the actual world and its obstacles, the person who can combat and overcome his inner anxieties will always move through life smoothly and forcefully. The crucial distinction between the two is that the latter recognises that these inner worries serve no existential purpose, while the former drowns in them as if they were an actual situation with a concrete existence.

You must acknowledge that your fears are your creation; because they are a reflection of your attachment to your past experiences and environment, and they are merely shadows within your psyche, not existential truths, and as a result, they don't have as robust of an impact on your life as you believe, your inability to move through life with ease is due to your incapacity to recognise and understand these fears.

Stop and think: You are unaware that you fear others' judgement about you and what you don't know, and as a result, you are constantly afraid of moving through life and taking steps that serve your growth.

Be aware: Stagnation is especially dangerous because it obstructs the flow of your life; the flow that is created by your willingness to move forward into many uncomfortable situations and circumstances that are by nature designed to challenge you in every aspect of who you are so you can broaden your horizons through these provoking experiences.

Free yourself: Challenges are what give life its meaning and purpose, and your ability to move through them is your constant challenge. When you become fearful, and the result of your fear is immobility, you essentially lose the fundamental purpose of your existence. Once you realise that the emotion of fear is yours and that you are the one who generates it, you will have taken the first step towards liberating yourself from your fear and beginning to break down the wall that you have built within yourself. It is crucial to establish the willpower to face your fear to be able to return to the necessary form of motion that is essentially creating your entire life.

Misperception

An individual spends his life defending his attitudes, expectations, and conduct, which serve as the foundation for the individual's vision of his life, attitudes, and interactions with others. These aspects are the filter through which one views life in its entirety because they construct his identity, essentially shaping his reaction to the outside world.

Frame your life: The essence of this filter lies in its emotional influence and effect because emotions are the compass that guides us towards what we desire and away from what we dread. Now that we understand the central role of emotions in how we perceive everything, we can see how fear can disrupt the processes of viewing life and reacting to it. If you are a person who is filled with fear, you are essentially experiencing yourself through this emotion, which you then transmute onto everything around you, creating threats where none exist, and as a result, you lose the ability to view and assess situations in their true light.

To connect the effects of fear on perception, we first must discuss its ramifications on one's view of himself; considering that this is the starting point for one's outward manifestations, a consistently fearful person's mind is always searching for flaws, potential mishaps, and worst case scenarios, it plots its own story with the finish line of failure, despite the irrelevance of this plot to actual situations and circumstances.

Think with me: Sometimes certain situations will have unfortunate outcomes, and this is an inevitable part of life; however, when you become entirely preoccupied and consumed with how bad everything can go, you become stuck with an interpretation of reality that is incorrect and negatively biased.

Be aware: this view will sabotage your attempts to fulfil your endeavours, your goals and desires will collapse, and you will destroy your relationships.

How to see the universe: You have to realise that fear may become a self-imposed constraint that significantly impacts how you regard yourself and your self-esteem.

Don't forget that we all have a dark side to hide, and also, there is a bright side. You must face the darkness within you to light a candle.

Remember that the presence of negativity within you indicates that sinking is imminent. This causes you pain, and over time, exacerbates your fears; it's a never-ending quest for balance between acknowledging your shortcomings and defects to be in a perpetual state of self-improvement and to continue to promote the bright, positive side to create yourself and this will allow you to blossom and shine in the world.

To be able to see yourself in the light of truth, you must first learn to get outside of yourself, your likes, dislikes, and your self-righteousness. Second, play the role of getting outside yourself so you can see what you face and the proper role you must take to discover who you are.

The truth of confrontation: This process requires a high level of acceptance of reality because we all like to think of ourselves as great, rejecting the idea of anything else, although facing yourself in this way can be painful, but if you have enough courage to do it. It will be such an empowering process, and this empowerment stems from the humbling effect of shedding light on your darker side and understanding your weaknesses, with this awareness, there will be a fire inside you that will try to overcome these unfavourable parts, and the fear will vanish since each negative aspect of you will become a possibility for progress rather than something to hide from and dread.

You must think in this way: If you are constantly overwhelmed with fear emotions, you are very likely to perceive situations with a heightened sense of threat and nervousness.

You may also find that even the most mundane daily events are fear-evoking. If you examine yourself and your emotions during such times, you will notice that fear emotions are essentially colouring your experiences rather than the other way around; the elevated feeling that you are experiencing tends to paint the reality for you, and as a result, your reality becomes obscured by a fog of fear.

Fear is a healthy emotion when a real threat is facing you because it protects you and increases your awareness so that you can act more instinctively to protect yourself.

Be careful: If this emotion becomes reactive to many non-threatening situations and becomes embedded in your psyche, your life experience will be severely limited and stressful, and your fears will colour many aspects of your life, including your relationships, where you will find yourself approaching your connections with others in an anxious and limiting manner, viewing the other through the lens of your fear and reacting to them accordingly. Your fears will make it seem impossible for you to set a goal and aim for it; and any time you encounter a new venture, you will be unable to fully experience it due to how the fear is focusing on self-protection.

Solutions

Acknowledging the Fear

Admit: The journey of life is profound and intense; it tests our endurance and pushes us to overcome our limitations and, as a result, expand our horizons; we discover that there is a constant challenge that must be conquered and a persistent lesson that must be learned. We are bound to experience fear throughout these experiences, and we can either make this confrontation a life-long struggle or an opportunity to deepen our understanding of who we indeed are and life itself.

Conquer your internalised fears, so you can liberate yourself from the many restrictions that impede your life experience and move to a new state of being.

Don't fool yourself: Often, our fears do not pass through our awareness, and we find ourselves overwhelmed with negativity and worry without realising the root cause of such feelings. Most of the time, we are the ones who create our fears to create inner hostility, and we make it a rule to move on with our lives. In today's world, our suffering lies in what we feel of stress and anxiety that has become a significant part of our lives.

We are unaware that these feelings will ultimately restrict our life experience and potential.

Fear has a destructive and unsettling impact; it is a negative force that has the power to destroy every aspect of your life because it becomes the driving force behind your actions and reactions.

Don't lose your tools: A person living in fear is limited, powerless, and easily shaken. If you allow your fears to control you, you essentially give up your conscious power of navigating yourself towards the path you want to take in life, and it's you allowing one emotion to shape who you are while letting your awareness of yourself fade away.

Admit your fear to break down your restrictive internal force; this is the most crucial step to take because it will allow you to interrogate your deepest fears; through this confrontation, you will be able to begin dissecting your fears and understanding their root causes.

Don't escape: It may be tempting to avoid such difficult and painful confrontations, but doing so will only keep you trapped in a circle of constant suffering and conflict because external situations will continue to reflect what you refuse to acknowledge and heal within yourself until you realise that all of the adverse conditions you are experiencing are guiding you towards awareness of your inner self.

Don't beat yourself up, and don't play the victim: where is your mind? Why should you continue to suffer when you can begin to work on your inner wounds and pains right now to live a happy and blissful life? It's always better to start this process yourself to gain the much-needed clarity and understanding rather than confronting this inner negative force through people and situations.

What you must do: First, develop your self-awareness by attempting to dig deep within your subconscious mind to understand the deep-rooted motives that lead to your actions and reactions.

Begin by examining your tools and your role as a member of a group and a community. And It is important to ask yourself, who are you? What do you love? Why? How? when? The fundamental examination begins with every external interaction because, in these situations, your reactions will come naturally, without any analysis or judgment. Part of your true nature will emerge through these interactions. If you pay close enough attention, you will be able to unravel many of your inner emotions and whether they are influenced by fear or not, but first, you must be able to confess to yourself that you are a person with numerous fears and limitations; if you refuse to accept your vulnerabilities, you will be locked in your fears simply because you refuse to acknowledge them.

Love or instinct: Consider whether your attachment to anything stems from genuine love within you or fear. Is it your instinct to respond angrily to particular situations, or are you attempting to safeguard something? Do numerous outside pressures suffocate you, or are you suffocating yourself somehow?

Through these questions, you may reveal a portion of your fears to yourself and begin your path of confronting and working through your fears. These questions may arise as you pay attention to how you act and react in everyday situations.

Remember that this could be a life-long journey because every new experience may reveal something about yourself that you have yet to discover, so you should always handle yourself with the utmost awareness.

Facing Fears

Now that you've recognised and developed a good understanding of the root causes of your fears and their manifestations through your actions and reactions, it's about time to start the next step you need to take to overcome them.

Select your goal: This process begins when you start focusing on facing what makes you uncomfortable. This is a fundamental step in the process of demolishing your fears and gaining a sense of liberation that is based on a solid foundation of courage through implementing conscious action towards coming face to face with what deeply scares you, you will be able to begin this transformational journey that will allow you to move to a new state of being, the constant confrontation between you and your fears will teach you how to get comfortable with what is uncomfortable and gradually get you out of your space of safety and security that is creating many of your fears.

Own your surroundings: Think of every aspect of your being, whether physical, mental, emotional or even spiritual, as a muscle that must be worked out and exercised for it to be strong and flexible. The process of consistent movement provides the chosen muscle with the strength and endurance required to function in an optimal, continuous, and powerful manner.

Remember that working on a weak muscle requires far more hard work and focus than working on an already strong muscle.

Consider this process to be a metaphor for what you'll encounter when you try to confront your fears; it'll be a struggle that requires a lot of conscious effort, devotion, and determination. You'll need to start with small, calculated steps, beginning with the little fears that usually stifle your ability to make decisions, take action, and create new measures, because if you start by confronting minor, everyday worries, you will gradually strengthen your bravery muscle, and that will give you a sense of accomplishment and progress.

Resist your fears: This should be a daily practice of attempting to accomplish something that makes you feel uneasy, terrified, or apprehensive. It might be as easy as greeting a random stranger or declining an invitation. If you have trouble saying no or expressing uncomfortable feelings, if this makes you feel uneasy.

Think of something small and basic that nonetheless makes you nervous. The key is that, while these exercises may appear easy, they ultimately connect to deeper fears, like fear of rejection, vulnerability, mortality, and a variety of other fundamental fears rooted in the human experience. The goal is to identify an activity related to your deeper fears and do it regularly. However, keep your approach indirect because you are not yet ready to confront your deepest fear.

Tear down the wall: After a while of doing your chosen exercises, you will notice that you are gradually becoming more courageous and willing to try new things that you know will arouse your fear, and you will also see that after each provoking interaction, you will feel satisfaction, happiness, and confidence.

Focus on these feelings, and embrace and accept them because you must nurture these pleasant emotions for them to grow and expand within you, eventually shifting your perspective on life and changing the way you see yourself.

When you notice that your exercises are becoming easier and easier, it's time to confront some of your more hidden and deep-seated fears; these fears will most likely manifest themselves in your more personal relationships because intimate relationships have complex dynamics that reveal many of your deep motives, desires, and fears.

This is a challenging stage because it will very certainly expose you to some painful realisations about who you are, your upbringing, and your past, which is never easy, and facing these anxieties will demand a lot of staying strength and endurance from you.

Breaking toxic fear-based relationship dynamics is exceedingly challenging since the process of rehabilitation and healing often involves emotional release, the establishment of firm boundaries, and, in some cases, the destruction of the relationship, which is always painful yet transformative.

The latter is more likely to occur if you live in an environment that is unwilling to cooperate and grow with you on this journey of the development of your subconscious mind, mainly because your environment is most likely to blame for instilling these fears in you as a means of keeping you under control.

You must prepare yourself for significant changes in your relationships and, most significantly, within yourself, since you will undoubtedly emerge much braver, with better boundaries and a stronger sense of self, as a result of this process because the primary purpose of relationships is to have a pure sense of unity and togetherness that supports your well-being and happiness, the people in your life should enrich you in many ways rather than drag you down with fears and anxieties, you must destroy all fears that relate to your connections with others.

Rationalising Fear

In life, we often get very attached to what occupies our minds. It becomes even more fundamental than our actual reality itself, although we can't deny the importance of diving deep within ourselves and our thoughts because this is a crucial part of actualising and manifesting our ideas in the real world. However, such involvement can lead to a disassociation with reality and its truths, where the mind disrupts one's ability to see things for what they truly are, for that, we must develop the awareness to differentiate between the actual reality of situations and circumstances and what the mind is exaggerating if you try to rationally think and dissect everything that you fear in life, you will realise that most of your fears are simply your expectations and thoughts and that you create.

Your constants: To be able to finally release all your fears, you must first understand the difference between an actual threatening situation and your psychological fears, you must apply this understanding to any challenging situation, where you keep your awareness that this is your emotion and not an actual danger. When you internalise this understanding, you will be far better at dealing with difficult situations because of your inner clarity and strength, which will have a significant impact on your reactions and how you handle yourself.

It is critical to keep yourself connected to the reality of things rather than colouring everything around you with your own opinions, views, and beliefs, and instead be able to detach yourself and just see. Because your entire life path is determined by how you see things, you should be as grounded and responsive as possible.

Conclusion

Your fears are there to haunt you, glaring at you through every encounter; you can either choose to comprehend and face these fears or keep them with you for the rest of your life; in many ways, it is a question of choice; you can either build a wave out of your battle or a prison.

You can use your fears as a bridge to reach a state of courage because one would not exist without the other; create motivations for you to find the opposite side of the same place out of your moments of fear and weakness; learn how to take control of the challenge rather than allowing the challenge to take control of you; transform your intense fear emotions by challenging and facing them to own your courage.

As my creation takes over, I live on trying to destroy what has become a part of me, and isn't it strange how a part of you can become your enemy? Did I need it to rise beyond what I knew, or was it my undoing? Many questions have arisen, but I know liberation is the only path for me.

A human

Sadness

Sadness is a feeling born in the subconscious mind due to changing influences and factors that affect the individual, thus stimulating his feelings with specific expressions. We know it through the change that occurs in the individual, expressed by sadness, misery, and pain.

We frequently utilise the word sadness to communicate a broad spectrum of intense and painful feelings that pierce deep into our souls and leave permanent scars in our hearts; however, the word itself frequently fails to explain the level of pain that we feel in times of loss and tragedy. Thus the purpose here is to genuinely delve deep inside its meaning and strive to unravel the depth of this feeling that we all feel throughout our lives.

The beginning of the story: The sadness in human life begins with the natural process of a child separating from his mother because the powerful attachment that is part of nature decreases as the child learns to become less and less dependent on the mother. This is primarily a human's first encounter with sadness. We can all recall a time in our childhood when we were deeply sad due to our mother's absence. The complicated concept tells us that we will spend the first years of our lives under someone else's care, but we can only grow by painfully separating from them; it's as if growth and independence are strongly associated with pain and sadness, that an attachment must be severed for a new, more vital form to take place.

Reveal your experiences: If you think about your personal growth, you will notice that the most painful of backgrounds and circumstances brought you the most growth and transformation; losses, tragedies, separations, and deaths are all pivotal moments that permanently change your life because of how much they impact your general views on life and its meaning.

The level of sorrow we experience varies widely from person to person; some people experience sadness momentarily as a reaction to a traumatic event, while others experience it more deeply and allow it to dictate their lives.

In both cases, sadness is a highly consumptive emotion because it casts a dark cloud over the person who is enduring it. A person who is experiencing sadness only sees darkness and is shielded from the light; he is filled with sorrow that nothing can heal; and if the feeling persists, it will transform into a whole new state of being that is dominated by hopelessness, loneliness, and a lack of motivation to live each day. Such condition can lead to attempts of self-harm and suicide, this proves the potency of sadness and how dangerous it can be if left unaddressed.

Explore the contrasts: Many paradoxes arise when considering the origins of sadness and attempting to comprehend its meaning: is it a part of life and existence, is it a testament to our humanity and ability to feel, is it the polar opposite of happiness that we must experience to reach the highest form of the same emotion, many questions, and many possible explanations can arise.

The main point is that every human needs to understand this emotion, as it is a normal reaction to difficult experiences and must be felt to some extent to maintain a healthy emotional state; however, it is equally crucial that we know how to cope with it and not let it cloud our lives.

Causation

Losses and Tragedies

Some moments represent focal points in our lives because of their significant impacts on our circumstances and the emotional residues they leave behind, such as success, failure, happiness, sadness, gains, and losses.

Such moments are marked by an enormous amount of change or grief and tend to colour our emotional and mental states to an undeniably powerful level. In a way, they become points through which we shape our life journey.

Losses: Have you ever attempted to define this term in your own way, to deeply contemplate what it means for you to lose, or have you followed the generally agreed-on meaning of this word?

We often forget to define and shape our perspective of the real meaning of a loss, we grieve what doesn't truly matter to us and discard what holds meaning in our hearts, and this leads us down the road of regret and late realisations about what we truly value and cherish which results in exponentially doubling the amounts of our grieve and sadness.

Each of us has his unique interpretation of what a loss is, but one definition that we all agree on is the loss of a loved one, the most painful and tragic loss of all.

Having someone with whom you have a solid emotional connection die is undoubtedly the most painful experience anyone can have, and it is by far the most challenging shock a human can face. Think about it, the end of life is the only definite end in this existence; everything else is renewable, changeable, and even reformable, except the end of life; as a result, when we lose a loved one, we enter a new understanding of our mortal nature that is difficult to fathom and accept, and this leads to unimaginable emotional suffering.

The scale: By choosing the individuals with whom we want to share a part of our journey. We contemplate the moments we want to create and share with them. We anticipate their presence and miss them when they aren't around; we essentially make an emotional connection that goes beyond the tangible and mundane domain of life, and this connection becomes a source of happiness, excitement, and even a driving force for our lives. However, we rarely consider how our life would be without them, how their absence would affect the tiniest parts of our days, how we do things, and the emotional void that their loss would leave behind, and even though death is an unavoidable part of life, we all struggle to accept it, and the feelings of despair that follow such loss are brutal and devastating, to say the least, because they lead us to lose our sense of purpose in life and make us despondent and uninspired.

Who owns the void: What we feel as a result of the loss of a loved one makes sadness a dominant weapon in our subconscious mind, and this feeling of pain increases after a while and our realisation that the one we lost left a great void inside us, so we surrender our souls to despair as a result of this loss, what pushes us is the enormous amount of love that we hold for the lost one, and these feelings become rooted in us and are difficult to get rid of, certain realisations can indeed help with coping and overcoming emotional suffering.

The most vital is to acknowledge that the majority of your sorrow stems from inner emptiness and void, as well as significant trouble grasping mortality, which is a part of our nature.

The essence of the problem: Another major issue that people face is their made-up definition of what a loss is, whether it's the loss of a lover, a friend, or any material possession, and while we do form strong emotional attachments to these essential aspects of our lives, our complete reliance on them to provide emotional satisfaction is bound to cause pain and misery, mainly when every unpleasant situation is categorised as a catastrophe.

Such an inaccurate interpretation of reality is bound to bring emotional suffering and distress; not to deny that life can be full of challenging situations, but there is a fine line between recognising the challenges a situation presents and exaggerating every distressing situation and turning it into emotional suffering and pain.

This is often denoted by some people's inability to regulate their emotions and develop a more constructive outlook on challenging situations; they prefer to view themselves as victims of life and their surroundings instead of working on facing challenges and healing their inner wounds.

On the other hand, those who have been in a continuous loop of dire circumstances develop a very negative outlook on any minor inconvenience that may occur because they are already in a negative emotional state, and anything could add to and blow up their pre-existing suffering.

While these are all coping mechanisms that people employ to deal with a variety of challenges in life, it is critical to comprehend and put each scene into context to alleviate some of your sufferings and avoid becoming the creator of your misery.

Expectations

Every day ends with a massive accumulation of gained knowledge and experiences we go through. Over time, we begin to notice patterns and repetitions in our lives and gradually rely on them to predict outcomes, to the point where we lose the ability to engage ourselves at the moment and instead rely on our instinctual alert to these repeating sequences.

Life cycle: In other words, we become unconscious of what sets up our emotional nature because anticipations and future predictions strongly influence emotions. The issue here comes in the fact that often, our projections, whether they involve another person's reaction, an outcome of a situation, or even a future plan, don't necessarily play out the way we expected, and almost always the result of this is a powerful feeling of disappointment.

Essentially, expectations lead to anticipation, and the nature of this anticipation determines what kind of emotion it induces. A positive expectation leads to excitement and enthusiasm; however, if the opposite of what is expected occurs, these positive emotions will flip to their opposite side of sadness, disappointment, and discouragement.

When we try to understand what an expectation is, we discover that it is one's prediction of a future scenario or outcome, a self-created prophecy that serves a personal purpose, and while expectations don't have an existential existence, they occupy a large portion of our minds and emotions.

We often identify ourselves with the idea of how things should be, how others should react, and how the future should be, and while it is vital to have a clear insight into how you desire your life to be, it is just as important to not lose grasp on reality by being attached to your expectations.

Think of it: If at certain moments, you lose your ability to control some parts of yourself, such as when you are angry, when you feel low, or when you cannot get yourself to do something you need to do, how do you expect others, situations, and life itself to unfold the way you want.

You must understand that every time you make an expectation, you are essentially setting yourself up for disappointment and sadness because every expectation is an unfulfilled desire that seeks gratification from external sources.

When the truth is present, the essence of what is lacking resides within you, and you must dig deep within yourself to understand the source of discontent and work on it.

I advise you: You must open up to life and the experiences it offers without modifying them with expectations because only in this way will you be able to involve yourself fully in the experience and gain the necessary knowledge and wisdom for your growth and expansion.

Live the moment and allow it to unfold its magic, give without expecting something in return, and most importantly, carry yourself with the utmost sensibility and care.

Once you drop down all of your expectations, you will be able to see reality with far more clarity and attentiveness, and you will come to see others and situations in their true light, which will allow you to flow through life with ease and joy.

Conflict

We always seek a haven that provides us with security, love, and understanding; it's one of the most important aspects of life for our emotional and mental well-being because we all need to feel understood and appreciated.

Since the dawn of time, we as humans have been formed into groups that can cooperate and build a life together, an organisation that serves a collective goal of living and expanding.

The beginning of this group is our inner circle, which includes our family and interpersonal relationships; this small group has a significant impact on our emotional state and mental health; a supportive and positive environment transforms our life experience into one filled with enthusiasm, love, and happiness, whereas a negative environment destroys our inner being and fills it with many negative emotions and sadness.

A life characterised by disputes and regular disagreements with others is certain to make us feel unsupported, misunderstood, and unloved, all of which are focal points in the destruction of our emotional wellness and clear grounds for overwhelming emotions of despair.

The root of the problem: First, we must comprehend why conflicts arise and what causes people to have such disputes and quarrels with one another because once we recognise the root causes of this unpleasant type of communication, we can begin the process of learning how to better understand ourselves and others.

The fundamental root cause of conflict is a difference, opposition, or clash between two individuals, which can be over a variety of things, such as differences in values, competition for power and authority, or poor communication. The one thing that binds all of these different causes of conflict is a lack of sympathy and understanding by one or both parties. When we look deeply, we discover that this is the part that ignites and accelerates disagreements because instinctively, when we sense that the other is unable to see our point of view, we quickly turn aggressive and defensive because we feel threatened and unsafe to express ourselves and our emotions.

Constant opposition in our relationships is bound to bring immense emotional stress and suffering because having to deal with a blocked form of communication in which the other is unable to extend to you an attitude of sympathy and understanding is bound to make us feel unappreciated, misunderstood, and unloved, on top of that, we become exhausted from having to constantly explain ourselves and fight for the message we are trying to deliver, it is as if we are entangled in a war that we cannot escape nor flee.

When combined, these many components result in overwhelming sadness and despair because recurrent confrontations with individuals near us make us feel lonely, alienated, and burdened by every encounter that may result in disagreements and fights.

Clash of poles: It is extremely unfortunate to live your life as if it were a battlefield, but what you must understand is the significance of these events and what they are trying to teach you because many times when you have conflicts with others, you sense the other person's aggression and lack of understanding, yet you tend to overlook your contribution to the conflict itself; we don't deny that some individual lack the tools for effective communication. However, to create healthy connections with others, you must be able to acknowledge your flaws in communication and understand the deep triggers that get you into conflicts in the first place.

Your weapon: It is empowering to consider how your actions and reactions affect the flow of events, and while this can mean many different things, sometimes you will realise that you are contributing to the chaos around you without even realising it, and other times, you will know deep down in your heart that the only right action is to leave the toxic situation for good.

Coming to these realisations will necessitate a great deal of in-depth analysis of yourself and how you interact with your surroundings, as well as others and their characters and everything that is contained within them, whether positive or negative.

Developing this mentality of being able to judge yourself and your actions in the same way that you judge others is a great point for many reasons; nothing is more powerful than holding yourself accountable for your actions and reactions.

Such an attitude will help you to extend the same sensitivity and compassion to others as you do to yourself, communicate more effectively, ease some of the suffering caused by such situations, and get a greater understanding of individuals and situations.

Consider this: Isn't it amazing to look at yourself as the focal centre of your life instead of drifting away like a boat crashing into the waves without a leader to hold its rein?

Memories

Think about how time passes and each second becomes a memory; isn't it fascinating that as the clock ticks, a memory is announced, and the future approaches with a present in-between?

It's as if we live our lives merging yesterday and tomorrow with a confused now; for yesterday colours how we feel now, and what we do is based on our desires for tomorrow. Most of us exist in this way; however, some people are emotionally and psychologically locked in the past since their identity and vision are both coloured by what occurred to them in the past.

Don't live in your past: We often find ourselves impacted by every situation we go through; it is almost as if we are an accumulation of our past experiences despite the differences in the experiences themselves and how we choose to handle and deal with them.

We are all conjoined by the fact that all of our past experiences reside in our memories, they become stored in our psyche, and we can access them whenever we desire. Memory is a crucial aspect of our existence because our memories are the storehouse of past information that we must be able to access to use stored information and data about the world around us.

The issue arises when an individual cannot move past a painful incident, he becomes emotionally and mentally stuck in that moment of the unfortunate occurrence. In such a situation, the memory is the place where all the repetition and recall of the traumatic experiences occur.

The mental remembering causes an emotional response similar to the actual incident, which is continually replayed in the mind. The crux of the matter is that in such a state, one becomes unable to connect to reality in its entirety but instead stuck in a mental cycle that repeats past experienced pain, and this becomes a source of powerful feelings of sadness and pain, and it even extends to a point where one begins to react to his current reality with the pain carried from the past.

How to think: It is essential to understand that human memory works uniquely. Many times something very random and unexpected could cross our minds, and other times we use the memory to stimulate certain emotions within us that are connected with past experiences, whether they were positive or negative.

Sometimes, we remember a beautiful moment only in hopes to get to reliving the pleasantness that we felt in that moment. Other times, we might recall painful situations to evoke pre-existing anger and pain.

The latter denotes that we are unable to overcome the pain felt in the past, and it has deeply scarred our emotions and how we feel; however, in both cases, the negative feelings are being stimulated by something that is not part of our tangible reality, and the central point is that we allow something that only exists in our minds to determine our emotional state, rather than trying to stabilise and harmonise our inner being according to how we want it to be and in flow with our surrounding and reality.

Break your chains: You mustn't allow past pain to control your present self or let it destroy your well-being; sadness in certain moments of life is inevitable, but if you take this feeling with you, you set yourself up for a life of sorrow and grief.

What you are asked: It sounds brutal and insensitive to tell someone to leave their pain behind and stop feeling the way they feel, as if it's an on-and-off button, especially if some painful experiences deeply wound the person. It is not a matter of not understanding and appreciating one's pain and suffering but a matter of learning how to process these emotions and finding a way to flip them to something that could potentially be useful in bettering your perspective on life, on how you can handle difficult situations, and how to move through life pleasantly and fully.

Separation

The true essence of life lies in its motion, and our ability to execute this motion determines the nature of our experiences. And life constantly moves us beyond what we know and understand, and our success comes through our ability to establish a renewed stability within us through every new step we take; this, however, demands a tremendous amount of self-mastery and strength that is not easy to achieve.

It is natural for us to struggle with any separation that could occur in our lives and to wrestle to comprehend the division between us and what love and value are.

Jump over the barrier: We have all experienced separation in a way that evoked powerful feelings of pain and sadness at some point in our lives. Being separated from a lover, family, or a place we call home can never be a pleasant experience because these events represent a moment of detachment from what provides us with happiness and security, and when we try to meditate on life and its motion, we find that it constantly moves us beyond what we've learned as a result of an experience because once knowledge is gained, an incident becomes a pointless repetition that doesn't serve our growth and expansion.

It's natural to move on to a new form of experience, the problem is that our ongoing need to find and maintain inner security stifles our drive to extend the diameter that confines our experiences, and as a result, rather than relishing new chapters in our life, we struggle and long to return to the same place that made us feel safe and secure.

Sadness, emptiness, nostalgia, and confusion will be present in your emotional state following the occurrence of a significant separation in your life, sorrow and emptiness are both related to the disappearance of the source of happiness that you previously had, and confusion comes about as you wrestle with sadness caused by the separation accompanied with the need to learn how to adapt and understand the new environment.

Get out of the loop: The separation in this situation will deprive you of your ability to fully involve yourself in the present because every separation marks the end of a chapter while an immediate new one begins, and suddenly you are forced to deal with both ends equally, and due to the collision of these two ends, adapting to and digesting this event becomes a protracted process that needs you to balance your inner self from the fusion of the past that you cherish and the new that demands your attention to discover.

Another aspect that heightens the difficulty of coping with these emotions is the perplexity related to attempting to find meaning within the event of separation because whenever anything that shakes the course of your life happens, you will most likely begin to question the reason and the purpose behind the event, the interesting thing, however, is that often the answers to these questions are never found immediately. Still, instead, they prevail through time and experiences that allow us to deepen our understanding of who we are and our lifeline.

Emotional pain is potent at the time of separation and continues until a new source of happiness is formed; you will be in a state of constant emotional ups and downs for a while, and the pain is described as a wave that rises without warning and is extremely powerful and destructive.

Change your life: This is a normal part of the process of adapting to the change that comes with the separation; however, you must understand that acceptance will be a significant factor in your ability to heal and progress through any problematic situation, and while we all have our expectations and hopes for how things will turn out, life is marked by a great deal of unpredictability, which you must embrace and accept.

Outcomes

Hopelessness

Hopes, dreams, and wishes, all have the meaning of aspiring for something that is beyond your current place and knowing that there is something out there that you desire to have, and this desire that we all hold deep within is one of the major driving forces for life, and it's what keeps our will to constantly take new steps and approach adventures.

Feelings of sadness frequently demolish our desire to move on in life; try to remember a time when you were experiencing powerful feelings of sorrow; you will remember that you had no desire for anything, that tomorrow was just another day to live, nothing to look forward to and nothing that sparks a spark of life within you, and it's unbearable to think about the future. These various feelings are all marked by hopelessness, a point in which one becomes so trapped by his pain that he becomes unable to see beyond it.

Destroy your wall: Hopelessness occurs when an individual's emotional pain takes over his being and isolates him from everything, creating a concrete wall around his vision and perception of everything; it's a state marked by a lack of inspiration, feelings of powerlessness, and helplessness, where memories become a dark reality that exists only in the person's mind and the inner pain feeds it constantly; passing moments become a burden and are filled with heaviness; and the future appears to be a continuation of the present suffering. This result of sadness destroys any good sentiments that one may possibly have about anything, including one's opinion of oneself, drowning him in negativity, shattering his inner self-image, and leading to excessive self-blame and hate, it's a point in which the mind becomes occupied with self-flagellation and the inner pain feeds of it and expands it, and this is a dangerous state to be in because if a person completely losses hope it can lead to acts self-harm and even attempts of suicide.

The primary reason why one enters a complete state of hopelessness is primarily due to his inability to see beyond his current suffering; when an individual is unable to see a tomorrow or a future without pain and sadness because he believed and surrendered himself to his pain, and because of his total investment in this idea, his pain exponentially expands and traps him in a spiral of the absence of motivation and desire to continue in life.

Don't play the victim: Understanding your inner pain and its level is essential. When your sadness reaches a high point, hopelessness will begin to creep in, and this combination combined with the absolute absence of any inner drive is perilous because, in a way, it's an internal death, a state of complete surrender to pain and suffering, as you allow your pain to take over you and your perception of life, of yourself, and others.

Isolation

Why are you shutting yourself away? What outcomes are you looking for? Why flee conflict and seek refuge in isolation? Is this your surrender to truth and the end of your life?

Cage: Whenever we are hit with a wave of sadness, we tend to withdraw and isolate ourselves from our surroundings, which can be a healthy behaviour and even rewarding if these moments are used for introspection and contemplation of the experienced emotions. However, when sadness becomes extremely powerful and consumptive, a person may experience a complete disconnection from everything and everyone, both physically (presence) and emotionally.

This state arises from the person's absolute inability to push through the inner pain; as it takes over his mind and occupies it entirely to the point where his ability to take action becomes paralysed because, for him, the only thing that exists is unhappy feelings accompanied by negative thoughts that repeat themselves, the result becomes difficult to break the cycle of pain, misery, and sadness. The longer this condition lasts, the worse the pain grows, and the more he becomes imprisoned by it; all of these different aspects play a key role in debilitating one's ability to maintain healthy connections, leading him to view every interaction with others as a considerable burden and unbearable.

Be careful: The most destructive part of all is the one related to the self-loathe tape that constantly plays in the individual's mind, for it repeats thoughts that lead to feelings of shame, unworthiness, and hate of oneself, and you can only imagine that a person of feels like this about himself is bound to be scared and burdened to interact with others.

The other possibility is that a person who is experiencing a great deal of sadness but is still able to go about his normal day-to-day activities, such as performing tasks, socialising when necessary, and generally keeping up with the pace of life. At the same time, the ability to be present and focused may mask the inner pain, but it does not eliminate it. It may sound ideal for one to motivate himself to push past his internal struggles, but such a coping mechanism has its drawbacks because if the inner sadness persists and does not improve through any activity, a person will experience emotional isolation, which is defined as an emotional disconnect with others and an inability to share vulnerability and emotion, and that will lead him to constantly try to contain his pain and put it in a box, pretending that it doesn't exist, which will eventually exponentially expands his inner suffering until he reaches a state of inner numbness.

This is a dangerous way to deal with inner pains and struggles because the denial one forms with his pain deprives him of his ability to deal with it and heal it, and since the state of constantly pushing one's self to function normally will make the person reach a high level of exhaustion, he will eventually breakdown emotionally and mentally.

It's crucial to be able to recognise the state of isolation that you may create for yourself, whether it's emotional or physical, and to comprehend its significance, because sometimes, in the chaos of the world and everyday life, solitude becomes a crucial part of emotional and mental well-being since most of our energy is constantly directed outwardly, which can often result in either inner chaos or emptiness. This state in itself can lead to many internal struggles and battles; however, it's also critical to surround yourself with a robust support system.

The part that makes others such a vital part of your life is the dynamic of bouncing back and forth, whether its emotions, thoughts, ideas, or general cooperation in life, as without others, this dynamic doesn't find a place to manifest, because, without the other, nothing can be brought out of you. No part of you can be challenged for you to grow; the mind runs in a continuous loop that creates patterns and habits that keep you in a cage, so to expand your horizons, you must open yourself up to others and the world.

Self-Neglect

To progress in the process of achieving your goals, you will need to work on all the different aspects that construct your life; however, the one factor that is the backbone to all potential that you can manifest in your life greatly depends on your ability to nourish and care for yourself, because without providing yourself with proper care, the foundation for all that can be becomes weak and unstable, and this is what we find to happen whenever we experience negative emotions such as sadness, we find ourselves unable to provide for ourselves the basics of what can make us grow and flourish. In this state, we neglect our needs and eventually grow mentally and emotionally weaker.

Don't surrender to your sadness: The nature of sorrow creates a perception blockage in one's ability to see a future free of suffering and necessitates a need for isolation from the outside world, these two factors combined lead to the last and final point, self-neglect, which is defined as a state in which an individual is unable to meet his basic needs in life. This inability may appear to be a lack of inner strength or drive, but in reality, it is a state of surrender to the emotional suffering that has been experienced, and this surrender occurs not because of weakness or fragility, but because of the limitation of human's capacity to deal with pain, and when this limit is crossed, suffering becomes a dark force that overtakes and destroys one's ability to let go of the past, feel the present, and have aspirations for the future. In this state, one lacks the urge to nurture or care for himself; in fact, in order to find relief from his suffering, he wishes to vanish and disappear from existence.

An individual who is experiencing sadness feels as if life is unworthy of living and that he is unworthy too; this extremely low state of emotions and thoughts in no way will bring the person to perform any kind of acts that could improve his condition, the pain takes control and deceives the person into thinking that it will last forever, so in this stage, the person feels no need to try and improve anything, it's complete imprisonment in which the mind constantly replays negative thoughts.

All of these aspects are highly debilitating to one's ability to perform all activities, especially those relating to any kind of self-support, as the person loses all kinds of interest in the things that used to be enjoyable before waking up in the morning becomes extremely difficult, eating habits may deteriorate. Basic hygiene gets completely neglected; this is the point at which sadness turns into a state of being that is characterised by dispiritedness, aimlessness, and agony.

Self-neglect: This is the final stage before doing any acts of self-harm; the emotional state can range from great inner agony to utter numbness; in any of these two states, the person begins to have suicidal thoughts. In some circumstances, a person commits acts of self-harm as a method to feel something because inner numbness can make a person feel as if he doesn't exist, while in others, a person seeks a way to stop his suffering, which in the person's perspective is to terminate his existence because life takes on the shape of suffering for him.

The essence of the solution: It is of great importance to develop a good understanding of yourself and your needs because only in this way will you be able to deepen your knowledge of your nature and what it needs, and more importantly, give you an insight into how you can provide and handle these needs to be in an optimal emotional state because many times we find that certain habits or enjoyments of ours change without us understanding the fundamental reason behind this change, and with this lack of awareness we unconsciously fall into unexplained emotional and habitual setbacks.

Solutions

Acceptance

Many distinctions distinguish each person's life since it is impossible for two individuals to have the same life experience; nonetheless, we are all bound by the exact nature of internal reactions to external experiences.

We all have to deal with sadness at some point in our lives because when we strip away all the outer layers we create for ourselves and enter the core being of who we are, we will find that sadness lies there in the fundamental human existence, no matter who you are, what is your place in the world, and how you go about living life, you must have had gone through times of inner pain and sadness, and the despite the differences in how each person chooses to deal with this emotion and what meaning they find within it, its experience remain inevitable.

Accept confrontation: To believe that sadness is inescapable is both challenging and freeing because it is not easy to accept the truth that part of life includes suffering; however, the more you embrace the reality of how unavoidable something is, the more equipped you are to deal with it.

The sense of acceptance you discover within yourself does not build a barrier between you and suffering but instead allows you to feel it with every part of your being without breaking down and losing knowledge of what this emotion is and how it affects you. As you come to grips with the fact that there is some suffering in life, you stop running away from it, and you eliminate any impulse towards denial.

Acknowledging and accepting significant parts of life is a mindset shift that will enable you to walk the walk of life with much more ease and stability, and when it comes to emotions like sadness, it is an emotion that we experience from the beginning of our lives.

Today you are sad as if you are still a child that hasn't grown yet, don't deny that the older you get, the better you become at handling feelings of sadness, which is an organic improvement because the more you are exposed to situations and circumstances that trigger this feeling within you, the better you can understand it and build strength when faced with it. However, mastering an unavoidable feeling should not take you half a lifetime.

The first step to accepting sadness as an unavoidable part of life is to examine your emotional state. Do you choose to isolate yourself from the world, feel compelled to talk about it with someone close to you, or stay in your environment but close off emotionally?

The primary purpose of this examination is to help you understand your unique attitude towards your inner pain and suffering and whether you accept it or flee from it. To take it a step further, analyse your physical state; do you have a stomach ache, feeling especially chilly, weary, and lazy? Concentrate on all of these emotions, sit with them, and let them run their course because only in this way will you be able to comprehend the actual effects of sadness on you and gradually begin to accept it once you give the feeling enough space within yourself, you submit to its nature without escapism or fear.

Acceptance also gives you the power to observe it in a way that gives you deeper insight into yourself and your being; that alone will enable you to become a genuine master of your emotions and their manifestation.

Believe your mind: The whole point is that facing your emotions is important because the better you understand how you feel, the better you can navigate your inner self in a healthy, stable way, where your consciousness is in charge of how you deal with your emotions rather than being ruled by turbulence, confusion, and instability.

Developing Strength

Many situations and circumstances put our endurance and strength to the test; some people gain strength by conquering these challenges, while others lose it.

Your weapons: Strength has been ingrained in the human mind and derives from the drive to survive, and it's truly astonishing to see how humanity has survived and grown to such an astounding degree.

On a more personal level, each person develops an extraordinary amount of strength through different experiences in life. Some focus more on the internal aspects of power while others focus more on the physical; what is impressive is that each of these aspects can have an impact on the other, where building strength in the physical body can result in a sharply focused mind while focusing on mental faculties can result in solid control over the body. In both cases, the point is that every one of us is always seeking methods to become stronger, more powerful, and therefore indestructible, and unshaken by the various storms that come and go on our path through life.

I remind you: When it comes to developing strength, emotional strength has to be the most dynamic, where a person who possesses inner harmony and composition is more likely to be able to deal with the difficulties that life may throw at them, especially those who trigger feelings of sadness and pain.

Inner stability and strength are the two elements that will help anyone get through any unpleasant situation; furthermore, experiencing feelings of sadness can be fruitful and beneficial because, through such emotion, one can learn how to sympathise with others and become more thoughtful.

The fascinating thing about sadness is that it hides a secret power within its folds, and that power is that only someone who has experienced the deep layers of human suffering can look beyond himself and feel for others because only he can truly understand the depth and profundity of others' experiences and emotions, and that allows him to extend an attitude of compassion without losing his inner stability and power.

Now the question is, how can you develop inner strength? First, let's define inner strength: It's the ability to maintain a stable emotional state without constant struggle and ups and downs of emotions.

It's important to note that having inner strength doesn't mean avoiding all the different emotions that one can experience; instead, it's the ability to recognise and maintain a sense of calm in the face of any aroused feeling.

Second, understanding your emotional state. You will need to cultivate a good understanding of your emotional state and what influences it; ask yourself if you are constantly fearful, always sad, or fuelled with anger. This understanding will be highly beneficial and will bring about a great deal of clarity, allowing you to change your negative state and move into a more stable and happy emotional nature.

Face your fears: After you have gained a sufficient understanding of the depth of yourself, you will be able to acknowledge your wounds, needs, and desires, allowing you to set boundaries between yourself and the things that trigger your negative emotions, which will be beneficial in building inner strength because creating boundaries will provide you with a sense of empowerment through the ability to own your well-being and general state.

It may be challenging at first if you are used to prioritising others' happiness over your own, but with enough effort and time, you will find yourself in a much better emotional state and as you begin to feel more in tune with yourself.

Paying attention to your inner voice is also highly essential for your overall strength and stability; how you speak to yourself determines many areas of your life; if you are always speaking negatively to yourself, you will be in a tumultuous inner state; and in a way, you will become your own worst enemy, and if you don't acknowledge this voice, you'll slowly destroy yourself with negative self-talk and self-flagellation. Quieting or muting this voice is anything but simple because this voice was most likely instilled in you at a young age; you've heard these negative phrases and words repeatedly until you've mistaken them for your own.

First, your key is acknowledging this voice because once you recognise it, you create a certain distance between yourself and what this voice is telling you. Second, use consistent positive affirmations to gradually fight back and change the nature of your inner voice to a more positive one, this way. Instead of concentrating on exhibiting a frail power that can be quickly destructed and destroyed by the outer world, you create a fort of unbreakable interior strength that radiates from the inside.

Third, dropping expectations is also very effective in reducing emotions of sadness and despair since if you live your life based on what you believe should happen, you will undoubtedly encounter numerous disappointments, which lead to many feelings of sadness and sorrow.

Your mark: There are many ways to begin building your inner strength, and while one method may be highly beneficial for some while being unhelpful for others, the vital thing here comes down to your ability to understand what is uplifting for you and what is your starting point; do you have a certain amount of strength and steadiness within you, or do you feel constantly shaken by every unpleasant event.

Be completely honest and transparent with yourself because this is your imprint in seeing the truth of things and yourself in crystal clear clarity, and this will be your strength in the storms of life that are unavoidable and might bring pain and suffering, there is no way out of these situations, but you can possess enough strength and poise to keep your feet on the ground and maintain your stability.

Finding Purpose

Define the motive: What motivates you to get out of bed every morning? Do you just start your day because you are alive, or do you have an inclination that is continuously screaming your name and urging you to follow it through?

Humans instinctively fight for survival; we are all eager to take place and continue with this life, whether we feel pulled towards a purpose or not.

Don't escape the confrontation: The fight for survival is part of the human psyche, and much turmoil and turbulence can diminish one's desire to continue; where the pain becomes too intense to handle, the urge to escape this pain settles in, and death seems like the only salvation, and although one might reach this condition as a result of experiencing a calamitous incident, digging deeper reveals that a lack of purpose within oneself can also lead to one's descent to such a low emotional state.

Select your goal: Finding your life's purpose is extremely powerful in elevating the nature of your life experience because when you discover something to which you are genuinely willing to devote yourself, something that creates a powerful force that governs the course of your life, you transcend with your existence beyond the mundane domain of life and enter a state of being that is deeply satisfying and rewarding.

Direct your force: Such a state will stabilise your energy and allow you to build a lasting legacy that will transform the lives of others instead of walking the walk of life scattered in many directions, confused, and unable to find your meaning.

The state of bewilderment that one enters when he lacks direction or purpose is a primary source of emotions of despair and worthlessness; we all need to feel needed and valuable to others, and when that doesn't happen, we feel useless and begin to doubt the significance and importance of our life.

Be constructive: This goes to show how important it is to contribute to your environment and society as a whole, where you help others and in doing so, you help yourself. Humans are always self-motivated, and denying this fact is a form of illusion, so it's always best to create your purpose in life out of something that you relate to and feel emotionally connected to while also having meaning and benefit for others.

This kind of thinking will help you include others in your goal, giving you a powerful sense of togetherness and strength; you will find that you are much bigger than what you've imagined, and you will stop thinking about what is in your best interest and start thinking about what is beneficial to whoever is involved.

Remember: Though it is critical to arrive at the correct judgement of what might be beneficial to the lives of others, it does not have to be a large-scale initiative that rescues mankind; it is just about giving value to someone's life.

Own the key: The link between finding purpose and the emotion of sadness is significant, and this significance stems from the fact that it prevents despair from reaching its highest expression, which is one's desire to end one's life.

The feeling of having something to contribute to will keep your motivation and desire for life high; although discouragement and sadness are unavoidable, having a purpose will keep you from sinking into a poor emotional and mental state, where you know that your existence is essential.

No matter how dim your light gets, it always shines bright again, in a way that makes you feel like something out there is holding on to you, and at a highly dark point in your life, this can be the only thread that keeps you alive.

Purify your soul: When you start digging deep and questioning the meaning of life, it indicates you need to move beyond the simple living manner of being and find a deep sense inside yourself that is channelled externally through action in the world.

This is a powerful stage to attain since many individuals simply exist, which is beautiful in its own right, but going beyond that means you have something to find and carry out that is intended for you to do, in a sense transcending your existence to a greater level of consciousness.

Expressing Sadness

We constantly seek new methods to express ourselves; expressing our identities, emotions, and thoughts is one of the essential things we attempt to accomplish in our lives; it helps us feel heard and seen, which is a fundamental aspect of our well-being.

But when it comes to emotions like sadness, they trap the person experiencing it with negativity and despair; what if the individual summons enough courage to channel their pain outward rather than inward?

It is often difficult to break through the barrier of one's sadness and find a way to express it outwardly, sadness has the effect of requiring isolation, and this isolation blocks all of one's actions and self-expression. However, finding a way to express one's inner pain can be highly beneficial.

The benefit comes from the transmutation of something happening internally into something tangible; as you put all of your emotion into action, that results in something you can see and touch. In a way, the pain and sadness take on a different form; it's not just an emotion that is trapped inside of you but a source for creation, which can ease the pain a little and give a sense of empowerment through the feeling that the intensity and complexity of the pain and sadness are being transformed into something tangible.

The possibilities for expressing one's inner suffering are numerous: writing a detailed account of how painful and enslaving these feelings are, making a sound that catches the essence of suffering, or painting a picture that tells a visual tale of grief; the possibilities are boundless, the goal here is to find an outlet for everything that is going on inside of you; choose a form of expression that you enjoy and use it whenever sadness overwhelms you.

Put every bit of how you feel in it and use it as a time to put your emotions into action; you will find that whatever you did, and whatever the results are, you will feel instantly better because you used something as an expression for your pain.

It's about finding ways to let your pent-up negative emotions seep out of you. Since most of these activities are done alone, you still have the safety of isolation that will allow you to go ahead and do the action without the presence of any outside pressure, so, by completing these tasks, you can keep your activity in a way that strengthens you through the pain that you are experiencing. You avoid reaching an incredibly low emotional state.

Although it's great if you can do an activity that results in creating something, this is not the only way to go about it; any kind of action that directs the flow of emotions outward is beneficial, such as a physical workout, journaling about your feelings and your current situation, or even doing a mediation to help ground and calm you down.

The point is to set up a time for yourself to make an activity that you intentionally connect to your emotional state, the connection that you create in your mind between these two aspects of who you are, emotions, and actions, is going to allow you to let out and release parts of these painful emotions that you are experiencing, and the benefit of choosing an activity that is not result-oriented is that it relieves the pressure of having to achieve perfection; it is simply about doing. You will need enough will and courage to break through the cycle of negativity that is imprisoning you, and in doing so, you recognise that you hold the key to your inner being's wellness.

Conclusion

The truth of human suffering is complex and paradoxical; some might even call it unfair; why do we need to experience pain? Are growth and suffering connected with one thread? Does suffering result from all our actions? Or does it represent the reality of the human experience?

There are many ways to go about this discussion, but the truth always remains present, and it is that the experience of sadness is inevitable; many situations, events, and circumstances will cause you to experience this emotion, and whenever you do, you will only have the option of fighting this battle or surrendering to it; it's your choice.

So what are you going to do? Will you use it as an opportunity to explore the deep crevices of your soul, or will you let it destroy you? There aren't many options with sadness, it's either kill or be killed, rise above or fall, and it's up to you to decide how you will go through this part of being human.

I questioned, wondered, and explored many times the road of agony; I got stripped away from all that is, fully knowing the result, yet still, it lured me in, a magnetic pull that I could not resist, was it speaking to me in its language, that I needed to understand, or was it my voice taking on a different tone, I still ask myself why, and the question is always there staring at me, will I ever understand, or is everything too present in a way, that makes me blind, the only thing I know is, that the power in me, shall always guide me through!

A human

Anger

The power of life lies in the essence of a person's movement and through which he achieves his goals. All is constantly moving, sometimes elusively, and other times forcefully; things meet and sometimes crash; this is the law of existence.

Looking at our human reality, we discovered that we possess a dynamic force within us, and we have come to know it in different ways through our experiences, with each person striving to achieve his goals and desires to be himself.

It's remarkable that many of us have had tremendous power but didn't comprehend it, didn't find its secrets, and didn't have the keys to mould it into its actual image and utilise it to convey all that is on our minds.

It is an extraordinary power when used correctly, but we discover those who have abused it and turned it into a devastating force for themselves and others around them.

We compare it to a knife that is best aimed at cutting everything it passes through, and although the outer exterior of this force may appear to be a possession of power, in reality, it is enslavement, not to anyone, but to a force within that is not correctly harvested.

An internal fire that can be your source of fuel, but instead, it constantly burns you down, causing friction between you and everything you come into contact with, and the result is that you will become a slave to the various compulsions and outbursts of the many expressions of this force.

Try recalling the many times you've been angry; they were moments in which you felt empowered but in an uncontrolled way; your strength was heightened, but explosively; in those moments, you said and acted exactly how you felt, with no filter, no veil on whatever was going on inside of you; you went about it with no thought or calculation, and in a way, you revealed a part of yourself that is hidden most of the time; a part that you don't want to see or confront, and that drop of curtains is filled with many questions.

Do these compulsions reveal a substantial part you constantly try to escape and hide? Or do they suggest that certain situations and people were provocative enough to manipulate your energy into transforming it into a dark monstrous form?

Both of these suggestions suggest negative aspects, first: that you possess some evil within you, and second: that others can control your being and affect you emotionally and mentally.

No one denies that anger is harmful and destructive, be careful, your rage is speaking to you in ways that you can't understand because you're trapped by it, but if you can calm yourself down a little, you'll be able to hear the authentic voice of your anger, and what it's trying to tell you.

Anger is only a mask you use to hide your fears; other times, it is a build-up of frustration caused by life-long unmet needs and desires.

Your anger is only an expression of what you hide, what is underneath it are aspects of yourself that you need to address and heal, and through the exploration and understanding of its dynamics, you heal and liberate yourself from the imprisonment of its compulsions, and direct your force to be helpful and constructive directions.

Causations

Hurt

The birth: We have all gone through circumstances in which we felt hurt, unhappy, and betrayed; we were deeply hurt, we cried, we screamed, and destroyed all that was around us, the agony pierced into our hearts and formed some kind of conflict within us, a war that required action, an explosion that needed to arise, or we would burn down in the fires of this torment.

Stillness: Each person has his unique way of dealing with being hurt by others; some surrender to the pain and allow it to run its course, while others transform it into an emotion that makes them feel empowered, one that will enable them to release some of their pain: anger.

The turning point: This transformation often occurs from the natural need to defend and by combining the inner pain with anger-triggering thoughts, such as assuming that the other person is intently trying to hurt them.

This combination results in a tremendous state of anger, which is undoubtedly unpleasant to be in; nevertheless, for the individual, it serves the objective of not having to cope with disempowering and painful emotions.

This may appear to be the best technique to cope with tough-to-process emotions because, in such a state, an individual's unpleasant internal state becomes focused externally on the one who created it instead of the experienced pain; nevertheless, the inner hurt still lurks beneath the surface of his anger, unresolved and therefore extended and unhealed.

The beginning of the problem: Anger many times serves as a mask of power; it empowers the person under its influence to act out some of his pain and suffering; however, this mask seldom addresses the fundamental nature of the experienced emotions, nor does it allows them to run their course. Instead, it becomes a way of reacting that dictates one's behaviour and reactions.

While outbursts of anger directed at others may provide a brief sense of relief and victory, they frequently lead to feelings of regret and shame later on, so when we dig deeper, we discover that anger creates a cycle of negative emotions that blinds the individual to his actual internal state and what it requires.

The loss of control: In moments of anger, one's perception of reality is distorted, and he loses his ability to make proper judgments about situations and how to react to them because he is trapped within the fire of his rage, and that creates a solid motivation to defend, attack, and create chaos, and this is what justifies the attacks on others and inflicting pain on them.

From your point of view, you see that what happened is a normal reaction because every action has a reaction, but you must remember that the nature of our responses has exterior as well as internal effects, and anger creates and reinforces aggressive behaviour that is immensely detrimental to your environment and inner self.

In most cases, the trigger for outbursts of anger are external factors, which are the cause of its explosion and harm to others, and we often get emotionally evoked unpleasantly, so the reaction is excessive and devastating, but it gives us confidence that what we did was normal and symbolised a method of rejecting everything that does not suit us.

Here the problem begins, and here is the birth of anger, with the repetition of provocations and the succession of their occurrence, feelings of dissatisfaction increase, and the reactions to them intensify over and over again. Hence, the compass of temperament deviates, and the silence and calmness that the individual was raised on fades from the subconscious to bring out the destructive giant who hates everything around him and everyone who opposes him.

The upheaval: Here, anger becomes a habit and acceptable behaviour by the one who does it, and it blocks his ability to sympathise with others and make proper judgments about situations, making the individual an enraged being who lacks the awareness to control and process his emotions.

When one uses anger as a tool to express the different emotions he experiences, he enters a dangerous state in which anger becomes a form of self-expression that leads to outbursts of aggression, so he harms himself and his environment.

Fear

As previously stated in this chapter, anger is primarily an external expression of a variety of hidden feelings and emotions, some of which are fleeting, while others are long-term, buried deep, and internalised within the realms of the subconscious, and we discussed how fear could be a significant trigger for anger in the chapter on fear.

The internal self is entirely interconnected; for it's the institutional circuit of the subconscious mind and its engine with many extensive layers that create a full circle that shapes the (I) that expresses emotions; many emotions are built around it and generated from it, and fear is simply one of those emotions that are internalised and inescapable because it is the key to express the rejection of a surrounding threat that jeopardises the (I).

The nature of a formed ego necessitates a constant need for validation, approval, and agreement, as these aspects ensure that the I is safe to grow and expand; however, when one is confronted with significant opposition or disagreement about a fundamental part that shapes who he is, fear gets activated, requiring the need to defend and protect the (I) from the perceived psychological threat, which often results in manifestations of emotions of anger, anger here is used as an instrument that allows the individual to empower himself, defend, attack, and sometimes even destroy the source of threat.

When we are fearful, the subconscious mind sends out stimuli in response to an eruption of rage, which manifests itself in one of the following ways.

First: a direct and destructive form that dominates one's emotions, behaviours, and reactions; it's powerful to the point where the individual loses consciousness of his state, and it frequently leads to rash and callous actions that are explosive and socially unacceptable. When we try to understand the depths of this state, we realise that it is essentially an internal declaration of war on whoever is attempting to destroy an essential part of one's self, a part that one cannot lose, so he searches for ways to protect and validate himself.

Hyper-concentration on self-protection and the destruction of the other distinguishes this state, but what is interesting is that fear is the true motive for this explosion out of desire and increased interest in gaining protection, and when the anger passes and the soul settles down and the causes of fear disappear, then comprehending what occurred is frequently overlooked and forgotten. One cannot see that what he did was not rational but a primal and instinctual image of a human.

Second: passive aggression: What happens as a result of strong external stimuli may sometimes reveal a significant weakness within us, causing us to retreat into our souls, carrying with us explosions that cannot be launched against the one who ignited them because he controls the balance of power, so we resort to ways and methods to express the anger buried within us, which moves silently like a volcano waiting to explode.

This type of rage is more damaging than the preceding one because it is characterised by intense feelings of dread and the urge to erupt. They are sentiments that are rooted under the surface and have not been exposed, and this is what leads many to see that person as being in control of his actions and able to command them, unaware that he is hiding behind the quiet that he appears to have, a volcano that will destroy him because it fuels his anger and heightens his fear and misery.

The categorisation of anger here shows a dimension of the psyche of individuals who experience fear and continual threat and volunteer to absorb shocks within a policy and method that goes with it, and arming themselves with this approach makes confronting and dealing with them challenging.

The primal part of the human psyche also plays a role in the conversion of fear into anger because the human fight for survival is deeply embedded on an unconscious level. It becomes the basis of operation for the many actions and reactions, so aggression becomes a necessary instrument, always ready to be used whenever it is needed. But that doesn't have to be the case all of the time; if you're constantly filled with feelings of anger that lead to aggressive actions and reactions, it's possible to raise your awareness and understanding to a level that frees you from having to experience such a negative emotion, allowing you to flow more freely through life and go beyond the primal aspects of survival.

Frustration

The nature of our inner force compels us to fight back against whatever is preventing us from pursuing happiness and fulfilment; it drives us to overcome obstacles and blockages, and anger is frequently the manifestation of this powerful human force that we all possess because it is both empowering and destructive; it allows us to demolish whatever is impeding us.

Frustration occurs when we are hindered from achieving our objectives and dreams due to an external or even internal source; internal blockages are often caused by an individual's fears, anxieties, and lack of self-confidence and belief in his ability to achieve his goals.

External sources include unpleasant life events and other people because those elements impact us and drive us to build hopes and ambitions for our success, and shock happens when those expectations are not realised, these feelings lead to anger, discontent, and frustration.

When the source of the blockage is internal, one's mind has a nature filled with negative self-talk, which reinforces any self-imposed limitations; this internal state often leads to frustration and annoyance, leading to anger.

This anger is frequently directed at oneself, where the individual beats himself up for his inadequacy and inability to achieve a specific goal, so he enters a spiral that saturates the pre-existing negative emotions; however, the interesting thing is that such state frequently leads to anger outbursts on others, because one's internal state is bound to impact how he experiences and interacts with the external world, so when one is frustrated and angry with himself, he'll very certainly react to the environment with a heightened sense of the same emotion.

When the source of the blockage is external, such as being stuck in a difficult life situation, one feels powerless and caught in a dark corner, therefore the force within rises in an attempt to revolt and break free, as a result, feelings of anger begin to creep in as a way of attempting to hide the frustration within. Here, one expression of anger is usually misplaced, because it is too powerful and it has the need to attack anything that crosses its path, one might even become angry with life in general, which transmute him into a complete state of rage that blinds his ability to assess situations and make proper judgments, causing him to act out with cruelty and aggressiveness, and while this veneer that is formed in an attempt to disguise the inner dissatisfaction and helplessness may continue for a while. It will eventually break apart as the internal force weakens, and one may even slip into despair and depression since the instability that distinguishes any extremism in one's emotional state consists of both a high and a low point, and in this situation, when one's frustration is unacknowledged, converted, and expressed through extreme anger, this is marked as the high point, and the fall becomes a state of complete hopelessness and depression, and if the blockage remains unsolved and present in one's life. It will create a paradox of rebelling and destroying that is followed by a complete surrender.

If the source of the frustration is someone in your life, this becomes an interesting topic because we often believe that people can block our desires in various ways.

Sometimes someone in our lives deprives us of our desire for peace and serenity; other times, people's extreme stance on opposing views or opinions becomes a significant source of frustration, and in many situations, someone's way of handling conflicts can drive us insane, there is a never-ending stream of unique situations where we're frustrated by the other.

To illustrate, when faced with opposition, aggression becomes a tool that one uses to assert power and establish and defend his point of view; if one is constantly confronted with negative actions from others, one becomes frustrated and, in turn, uses anger to inflict the same pain on others, which is an act of revenge.

However, when a loved one cannot sympathise and understand us, we get furious and defensive; in reality, we are merely masking our scream for love and compassion.

These are different scenarios with one common thread: how can frustration lead to aggression and destruction in our relationships with others, and what must we do to better understand ourselves? We must dig deep within ourselves and not let our initial emotional reaction delude us from the profound truth within who we are.

Ego

Think about who you are. What are the elements that distinguish you? What is their essence? And what is it that genuinely gives them their meaning? You will discover that many of the things you label as yourself are either sets of ideas, philosophies, or accomplishments that give you a sense of empowerment and value.

We all feel the need to connect ourselves with something greater than who we are to feel strong enough to face the world; however, by doing so, are we creating an illusion that has no link to reality, or is this the only way we can increase our self-confidence and belief?

Self-identifications are the characteristics that we see as ourselves in our conscious mind, as opposed to what lies underneath in the realms of the unconscious, which contains all of our prior experiences that mould and develop every component of ourselves that we are oblivious of, such as our innermost motives, fears, and wants that we mainly don't recognise and acknowledge.

Now, the ego function is essentially what we view as ourselves; how we experience ourselves as the I, the identity, enables us to separate ourselves from the outside world, which is an enormously important aspect of experiencing ourselves and life in a normal, healthy manner.

When an individual becomes entirely engrossed in the I, his experience of himself becomes what he is most aware and cognizant of; his ideas, feelings, opinions, and beliefs become his most important possession. The individual's perspective becomes blocked by all the aspects that he perceives as himself since his complete self-absorption restricts his capacity to investigate others and external influences.

The process of research and review only takes place to confirm one's identity and in a unique way that only searches for what might add to his pre-existing sense of superiority and grandiosity, and once this inspection leads to one concretising his beliefs, one begins to find ways and methods to constantly establish and protect them.

What happens next is that one's experiences become filtered through these idealised beliefs that are constantly in need of establishment and protection, so he begins to approach situations and others from a place of righteousness and grandiosity that further inflates his ego, ignorant of the presence of others around him, confirming that he has reached perfection and denying the existence of defects in him, in a way, one becomes blind to his truth and the truth of others.

To where we arrive: The question that comes to mind is how the ego can be one of the main contributors to the emergence of feelings of anger. Consider this: if one establishes a heightened sense of superiority within himself about who he is and what he believes in, combined with a complete and constant absorption of all of these aspects, he is bound to be filled with feelings of anger whenever confronted with any kind of opposition or objection.

The reason is his sense that he is, in fact, superior to others, and that gives him the justification to attack and disparage everything different, anger becomes a weapon that is used to safeguard and establish the stance of power that one feels inside oneself.

The ego is never satisfied and always wants more, which drives a person to impose his laws and beliefs on others without being receptive to their points of view and opinions. As a result, one loses his ability to grow his knowledge and deepen his understanding and even become blind to all of his flaws and mistakes, making him unable to acknowledge and resolve any of his wrongdoings and problems.

Constraint

Have you thought about the ceiling of your freedom? And how would you describe your feelings now that you're free? Did you try to deconstruct all the constraints you've imposed on yourself, the limitations that keep you from experiencing your true self in its purest form?

We live our lives with the illusion of having freedom when in reality, we frantically seek to create walls around us that make us feel safe and comfortable, believing that this way, we can have a sense of security while also getting on the edges of these barriers to have some sense of freedom. Still, the truth is that we end up being confined, and we live our lives with a lingering sense of continual restriction that haunts our dreams and desires.

The interpretation of our cohabitation with freedom is frequently disregarded, which provides the limitations that lead to the outpouring of anger and its lack of recognition.

We acknowledge that the law of the universe imposed itself and confirmed its aspects through an equation to create a balance between humans and the imposition of restrictions through force and authority. Violation of the balance equation created limitations on the individual's freedom and placed controls on his behaviour, which led him to a dead end and caused an explosion.

Imagine a scene where two opposing powers, each possessing the same amount of force, collide at one point, fighting over who will move the other, and as the battle progresses, both forces grow immensely, but only one can completely blow the other one away.

It's the one who resists long enough while maintaining the same persistence of the flow of power and force; understanding this dynamic can help you understand why each one defends to gain his freedom.

Emotional constraint occurs when a person is overwhelmed by various emotions but unable to express them in any way.

The reason is the programming that reinforced the repression of those feelings early on in life; such individuals were taught that their emotions are unimportant and that expressing them is rejected and burdensome to others, and that pushed them to keep their feelings to themselves and put them in a box, so they lost their ability to express and share complex emotions.

They grew up, and anger turned into a way to break the constant emotional constraint that prevented them from expressing the truth of how they felt. Anger here was used as a declaration of rebellion against the inner force constricting and inhibiting them.

We can imagine this situation as two polar opposite energies within one individual, one resolving to silence because it protects, while the other yearns to break this silence and express its truth.

The other way the dynamic of imposing constraint can manifest is through the laws that restrain the behaviour of an individual, where one finds himself in extreme opposition with an outside source, whether it is an individual or the imposed societal rules and structures, a human's desire for freedom and his desire to enjoy it are what drive him to battle against anything that can pose a danger to its realisation.

Some might say: For what is the point of one's life if he cannot act of his free will? This question is supported by the reality that there will be no other way to challenge the law but through opposition, rejection, eruption, and rage as an effective method of triumph.

This tactic might be completely primal and animalistic because it goes beyond all that makes sense and all that is rational, as an individual's freedom is connected to something that is deeply existential, and it touches on a deep core part of his psyche, and this explains the numerous fights and wars that have occurred throughout history concerning freedom.

On a more personal level, most of us have had to fight other people or authority figures for the belief in our right to freedom of choice, and what distinguishes these situations is the tyranny of explosive destructive anger over the language of the mind and at these moments a human is ready to risk everything, for our instinct resists and will not allow anything or anyone to take away her most valuable possessions.

Outcomes

Destruction

Connections are an intangible extension that ties two components together; in a sense, they are part of the profoundness of life; after all, everything is connected in ways that go beyond our limited human comprehension, and your connection to everything and everyone will have a significant influence on you since what you extend to what is beyond yourself is sure to return to you in many ways.

If you have a powerful force within you that's in a state of extreme chaos, a calm fire that is waiting to erupt in a lawless matter, it's unmanageable, undisciplined, and violent, you are bound to own power, the power of destruction, for you are saturated with anger, the feeling that is controlling you in many ways, and you find yourself unable to manage or control it.

We are constantly trying to rise above what already exists in our lives to build something that provides us with a sense of satisfaction and security, and we create our identities, connections with others, and careers that give us a sense of power and usefulness.

As we've mentioned throughout this book, our emotions heavily influence all aspects of our lives, and a strong emotion like anger is bound to affect you and your relationships with others because when you are filled with feelings of rage and anger, it is a sure bet that these emotions will be transferred to others with whom you have a connection because your internal state determines the nature of your reaction to the outside world.

Anger is the manifestation of a powerful human force that is connected to one's inner drive to survive, his primal animal that is a pure form of energy, and when this force is mixed with anger-triggering thoughts and emotions, a person here is influenced by this powerful force that is uncontrollable and destructive. However, it is primarily destructive not because of its experience, because feelings of anger can be highly beneficial if channelled and harvested in the right direction, but rather because of the way one becomes a slave to its compulsions, developing a defensive attitude that views everything as an opportunity to create conflict in order to release some of the pent-up anger, such an attitude becomes focused on inflicting pain on others, and this is what leads to destruction and ruin within one's relationships, because the individual loses his ability to sympathise with others' emotions, understand their different perspectives, and review where they are coming from, and others become a source for feelings of anger to feed on, which frequently leads to explosive fights and quarrels in relationships.

Although an individual may experience a rewarding feeling of power when exploding in such situations, mainly if this person's anger stems from issues of control and feelings of weakness, such a feeling is often fleeting and does not acknowledge or solve the internal problem that one is experiencing.

Everyone has their degree of endurance, and one can only take so much pain from someone they care about, so having an emotional connection with someone means you will be significantly affected by them, as there is an emotional investment and attachment, so insults, emotional abuse, and disrespect all result in resentment on the other person's side as they become imprinted in their mind, and that in itself is very likely to turn the relationship into eremitism.

Chaos

Have you discovered the secret concealed inside you that generates chaos? The one you can't seem to understand or control, and whether chaos is a temporary phase in your life or a continuous pattern that plays itself out, do you fall back on blaming outside circumstances and using them as a justification for your failure to establish order in your life?

Anger is an interacting outcome of several internal or external influences because an angry person cannot discipline himself, as his thoughts, emotions, actions, and reactions all become scattered in many different directions, leading him to the path of vengeance, hatred, restlessness, and destruction.

Being preoccupied with all of these aspects at the same time as a result of angry emotions will eventually result in complete disorder and chaos in one's life, beginning with his inner state, which is what sets up all of his exterior manifestations that are accountable for the formation of his life's structure.

When feelings of anger pervade every aspect of your being, you become so engrossed in the emotion that you lose control. As a result, clashing becomes a repeated theme in your life, making you more defensive and easily drawn into conflict and disagreements with people, and you lose your capacity to focus on essential things and make effective decisions in your life.

Such a state usually indicates unconscious traumas that push the individual towards destruction and disorder. While an individual may want peace and harmony consciously, his unconscious and unacknowledged wounds produce a far more powerful motive that drives him down the path of disharmony and aggression.

An angry person's energy is frequently scattered in a variety of destructive directions; he misplaces his anger on various people and circumstances and may even become angry at life itself, triggered by minor inconveniences; he enters a complete state of internal chaos, which leads to irrational and explosive reactions. However, the interesting thing is that in this state, an individual is unaware of the root cause of his emotions, and he misinterprets the source of these deep-rooted feelings for what he chooses to direct them at, which are frequently only stimulants that touch on parts of him that are unhealed.

Lacking awareness, an individual is easily triggered and reacts with extreme and aggressive behaviour, only to realise later on the banality of his reaction because his reaction was triggered by a portion of his unconscious mind that holds unhealed wounds from the past.

The major driving force behind this eruption of anger is chaos, which causes the individual's response to be magnified in comparison to any average effect; this is bound to cause an enormous amount of chaos and disorder in one's life, as one's inner state is unstable and constantly shaken by minor things.

When you are easily triggered and affected by everything, you lose your ability to focus, prioritise, and sustain many aspects of your life.

Cycle of Regret

Much like war, the emotion of anger has the same effect of absolute chaos and destruction, but in a different form, one that is psychological and meshed within the cracks of the human psyche, that contains all of the polar opposite traits of good and evil, constructive and destructive, obedient and rebellious, and within these polarities, we find ourselves constantly moved in a state of confusion, from all of the divine virtuous attributes we believe we possess to what we most dislike and abhor, it's almost as if we carry both good and evil seeds within us. This continual oscillation between two polarities will inevitably lead to feelings of bewilderment, shame, guilt, and regret.

Once the effects of one's rage have subsided, he gradually returns to his usual level of consciousness, looking to assess the damage he had inflicted while reviewing the time when he lost control and caused so much harm. An individual's emotional state gets slightly muddled at this stage because the return of consciousness causes the individual to justify his actions and wrongdoings, but regret and remorse eventually creep in.

Feelings of shame are associated with emotions of sorrow and embarrassment due to one being conscious of his wrongdoings. On the other hand, anger causes a loosening of one's moral boundaries, allowing one to cross lines and harm others.

What connects these two emotions is that anger allows the individual to feel empowered enough to act aggressively and violently, and it is this aspect that will enable one's internal aggression to manifest; however, as the powerful feelings of anger fade, one begins to realise the wickedness of his actions and reactions and that they were unrepresentative of his character and intentions, forcing him to go through the process of self-judgement, which is filled with intense feelings of shame, as one cannot comprehend all of his horrendous actions and reactions, what's intriguing is that what fills this judgement with all of this emotional turmoil is the fact that it's made from a different level of awareness, one that isn't obscured by heightened emotions that create the impression that destruction is necessary, reasonable, and justified.

Regret and guilt are also included among the after-effects of anger outbursts, as these two emotions are part of the self-reconciliation process. Regret prevails for two possible reasons: one is related to the damage that was done to others, in which case a person realises his wrongdoing and regrets his actions, though the level of regret one might experience considerably depends on how redeemable this damage is, and if a sincere apology and a change in behaviour can remedy the problem, this may dramatically reduce emotions of regret; but, if the damage was irreversible, such a circumstance might result in life-long regret. Therefore, it's critical to be mindful of your actions and their consequences. The other side of regret is triggered by reasons related to the I, when one feels that he has ruined and wrecked his self-image, went out of his usual way and lost control over his self-control, and revealed a part of himself that he would rather not face; neither sympathy nor guilt is genuinely present within this person's emotional state towards others and the pain he inflicted on them, as his only concern is his self.

When one becomes vividly and fully aware of his acts and their consequences, of destruction and ruin, and a breach of his own or universal moral norms, guilt emerges, bringing with it a certain amount of inner suffering and torment, as one wishes to go back the moments of harm to alter the courses of his actions and make better choices.

The greatness of time is that it can only go forward; every word and action spoken or done is like a shot from an arrow; once fired, it cannot be reversed; nonetheless, the experience of a painful emotion such as guilt has excellent effects, as here an individual learns to become more thoughtful and compassionate to bring about some sense of inner peace and relief to such feelings, the pain has a more profound influence than anything else, it pushes us to discover discipline, sympathy, and awareness that improves our moral standard to the point where we become wholly committed to the welfare of others rather than bringing them hurt and misery.

Solutions

Realising the Source of Anger

Knowledge is the light we constantly seek in our lives, and when we search for it, we embark on a journey that must lead to enlightenment, for we effectively open ourselves up to a life-altering expansion that will empower us to take control of our destiny.

Know yourself: Your eagerness to know yourself will be your way to healing the deep crevices of your soul, you are the master navigator of your life and your limited time on this planet, and to create the life you desire, you must learn how to create harmony and strength within yourself, which is the highest level of mastery one can achieve, and it is what will allow you to flourish beyond all limits and obstacles.

Discover your flaws: The eruption of anger emotions causes the individual to lose his self-control and the recurrence of external stimuli that elicit feelings of anger and nerve loss results in the release of pent-up and concealed emotions; this situation frequently arises as a result of one's lack of awareness of how triggering altercations truly affect him.

The key to overcoming this state is for one to develop the ability to grasp the point at which he was triggered, as this is a crucial point that reveals to the individual the source of his anger and also allows him to manage the aroused emotions before they escalate into unpleasant and destructive directions.

The main question is how one can catch the subtle moments of annoyance that serve as the soil for an emotion like anger to grow and expand.

Own your tool: You must learn how to tune yourself to your emotions and their physical effects; when you tune yourself to both of these fundamental aspects of who you are, you raise your level of awareness to the point where you can understand the root causes of your emotional reactions.

To better understand the root causes of your anger, pay attention to the small things that irritate you, what they are and how they make you feel. Are you experiencing any physical sensations as a result of these feelings? To demonstrate, did someone's opposing opinion ruin your day? Did you become irritated by a negative comment? And most importantly, how did you interpret these situations?

These various questions and observations serve as a starting point for you to increase your level of awareness and understanding of yourself, allowing you to gradually overcome your impulses and cultivate better self-control.

Another moment you must inspect and understand is when you become defensive; stay alert to how you react to others in such moments and how the argument is progressing. Are you becoming more aggressive, or is your vocal tone gradually increasing?

These are all signs of anger that you can detect in yourself and others; in such situations, you must learn to resist the urge to prove a point or win an argument because this desire will cause you a lot of emotional turmoil and waste time and energy. Instead, remember that the actual victory is in your capacity to compose yourself, not in wasting time and energy on trivial fights that serve no one; it is in you being aware of how to own your power, and knowing where to focus your energy and attention.

Discover your hidden secrets: Consider this a process of inspection, in which you begin to look for subtle hints and clues, heightening your level of awareness of how you function as an individual and as part of a group, looking for what triggers this feeling within you, whether it's a specific situation in your life, an individual with whom you can't seem to get along, or even yourself.

Look for the root, the starting point, for this is where the change and improvement must occur. Otherwise, you will find yourself constantly trapped by this emotion, unable to free yourself from the many obstacles and difficulties associated with your inability to control yourself and direct your energy in the right and constructive direction.

You will also notice that as you begin this process, there will be a drop in anger that is purely related to this analytical approach, as you stop being wholly involved in the emotion itself but instead observe it and its progression, even throughout its experience, you try to be aware of its how's and whys, this will disrupt the complete absorption that we tend to experience with our emotions, which will tone down its potency and power that it has over you, and through that, you will be able to calm the storm down and develop the ability to have complete control over yourself, in its complexity and wholeness.

Accepting Differences

Our identities form based on the various values, beliefs, and traits that exist, and it is through this formation that we can go through life with a sense of clarity and strength; it also allows us to lay the foundations of our life path, which includes distinguishing between what we want to associate ourselves with and what we choose to completely exclude from our circle.

An instinctive purge that allows us to find allies and identify foes; however, this is simply a search for comfort in what feels familiar, which reinforces our fear of the unknown, evoking a variety of negative emotions, including anger, because of the need to maintain a powerful stance within our circle of beliefs will demand a bold kind of reaction against its opposite. This action often consists of an internal force activation paired with angry thoughts and emotions, forming a powerful union capable of establishing a place while belittling and destroying the other.

We appear to have lost our capacity to accept others who have different values, our opposites who also possess the same power of belief as we do, because we are constantly so engrossed in what we know and what defines us that we forget the diversity and complexity of each existence on this planet; it is a type of ignorance that dominates our being that we cannot seem to recognise and grasp because if we can look beyond ourselves, our desires, motives, and what we take pride in, and open our eyes to life in its entirety, we will find breathtaking magnificence that goes beyond what we can ever be or create.

In a way, it's about realising that we are only a tiny part of this grand universe and that no matter how much one can accomplish, possess, or even create, he is still a small fraction of the greatness in the universe.

Arm your mind: Such a way of thinking will be of tremendous assistance and value to you, on all scales and in all aspects, for your welfare and capacity to broaden your horizons to realise your full potential, since only by recognising how small you are will you be able to look around you and see the splendour that exists in everything and everyone, with the hope that through every contact, you will be open enough to fully experience and be affected by the beauty that is there.

You must learn how to nurture your capacity to stand firm through the many oppositions that you may encounter in life, and that many times individuals will have different nature of views, opinions, and outlooks on life, and that is great. Acquiring the grace of acceptance will offer you the capacity to look at the world with open and clear eyes, and to keep your curiosity alive towards what is unknown to you, rather than being intimidated by it if you don't learn how to develop this skill, you will end up living a life confined by the tiny amount of information and understanding that already exists inside you, imprisoned by your ignorance and fuelled by an emotion such as anger to be able to cope.

Stillness

When you reflect on your past and the many situations you've encountered, you'll notice that each step you've taken had a different possible outcome. Much like standing on a two-way street, each road contains an entirely different world of possibilities and difficulties.

Every move you've made has led you to where you are now; through this examination, you'll discover the map of your life, including why, how, and when everything happened, and which decision led to which outcome. But, more importantly, you will realise the power you have in navigating your life. What's interesting is that many times, we are emotionally influenced by our environment which ends up shaping our actions and reactions. However, we often fail to realise that this continual movement and mobility defined for us by others is sure to bring an enormous degree of instability and shakiness into our inner world and our power to construct our reality.

What can be very helpful in eliminating anger emotions is to learn and understand stillness, both as a concept and as the starting point for all motion; if one has mastered stillness, he will develop a nature that knows when to move and when to stop, when to react and when not to; its understanding when to direct your energy and when to save it for more constructive and dynamic action.

Learning to be still when you're filled with anger isn't easy. It'll require self-control at first, but not in the way that leads to the explosion, but in the way that calms it down, where you stop yourself from acting out in a moment of lack of awareness, which may be difficult, but it will undoubtedly save you many feelings of regret and shame that may follow an outburst of anger.

It is about learning to control your compulsions to overcome your destructive impulses. The question that now arises is how, first and foremost, you must learn how to develop the ability to assess the situation that is presenting itself to you, what the situation is about, what is triggering your anger, and what is the dynamic in play between you and whoever is involved are all critical questions that you must learn to answer, as they will be the determining factor in bringing to life your ability to have the most significant amount of control over your anger impulses.

The first point that is mentioned earlier is understanding the root cause for such emotion and the central point in containing it; after that comes the analysis of the general situation and its significance and importance, as many times in your life, you will find that you are involved in situations that at the moment feel critical due to how emotionally moved you are by them. Still, only through the passing of some time, will you be able to look back and come to the realisation as to how insignificant and pointless these whole situations were, and this proves the necessity of having the proper evaluations for what is of significant importance to you, that is worth spending time and energy on, and what is only a passing inconvenience.

This way, you will be more than willing to move out and not give in to many pointless arguments and disagreements because this understanding will begin to come to you faster than before, and through time and developing awareness, you will see how many past issues and problems have cleared out of your life.

Your closed circle: now, the next step, which can be ranked as the most important, is to understand the dynamic between you and your environment. Is it triggering you constantly and pushing you to the edge, or is it of a supportive and understanding nature? This is extremely important, even though the goal is to create inner harmony and stability despite external conditions and circumstances but to be able to take the steps on that road, you will need to have some form of cleansing of many aspects that are triggering in nature, especially within your circle, because if there is someone who possesses a destructive streak. It will be challenging to break the cycle of destruction, without creating limits and boundaries, that enable you to draw the lines on what is okay for you and what is not, through this process, you will be able to acknowledge the behaviour that you find to be unacceptable, and that triggers your negative emotions such as anger.

Going through these steps, you will be able to realise and understand when to implement your actions and when to remain still and not act nor react; you will be able to contain yourself in moments of anger and be aware of the heightening of the emotion, where it is stemming from, and whether or not your surrounding contribute to the rise of it or not, all of these aspects are incredibly beneficial in helping you find stillness in moments of eruption.

The source of enlightenment is understanding that will bless you with inner clarity and help you to control and balance yourself; you are no longer lost within why you feel this way, you know, and now, you can untangle all of your inner complications, so that you become aware and keen, in every action that you take.

Redirecting the Force

How we live is entirely our choice, and what we encounter is a truth, not an accident or an absurdity, yet many of us have failed to recognise that established truth. With the absence of awareness, every emotion that we experience is like one surge that has no source nor a direction, a clutter that takes over, consuming every inch of our being. It's best described as a state of complete loss within the inner battles that are constantly reoccurring due to outside forces and circumstances.

The power of anger, if redirected, can be of great benefit; as mentioned earlier, it's a force that many times gets misplaced due to its sharp, explosive nature. To become conscious of it, aware of its roots, and able to express it in a different direction that is not of a destructive nature, without causing harm or damage to your inner self, or your surroundings, you must develop an awareness of the level of anger that is possibly going to lead to an outburst, and just right before that moment, choose to withdraw from the situation you are involved in, take a moment of solitude and silence, and then proceed to follow it up with an activity that you find relaxing.

Search for an activity that allows you to release your anger; it could be a physical workout, a walk outside, or even a grounding meditation. The choices are endless.

The goal is to navigate the emotion and its need for expression in a different constructive direction; you use the activity as a momentary primary focus, bridging it to your feelings so that it becomes an extension of it, which is what fundamentally allows the release to happen, through this redirection, you stop any engagement that helps your anger to grow and explode. You also entirely shut yourself off from acting out in a moment of disturbance and fogginess. You will also find that as soon as you have finished the chosen activity, your perception of the general situation that has caused your anger has changed because, many times, the urging need for self-expression can play a significant role in heightening the emotion. Its explosions, so fulfilling this need in a different form will allow you to build positive habits out of your negative emotions.

Conclusion

An inner fight, an urge that is difficult to control, to establish power, find safety, and fulfil desires, emotions of anger: are they an expression for a painful internal battle? Or a primal aspect of our nature that is brutal, uncensored, and destructive?

Many suggestions can be presented, but only the truth can stand tall; the reality of anger and its existence cannot be hidden nor ignored; it is there, within every one of us, imprisoning some while motivating others; it's a matter of choice, perspective, and self-awareness.

Do you live in the current moment to overcome challenges and achieve inner stability? Or have these constraints imprisoned you? It's your life, your existence, that demands you to take the necessary actions to achieve success, happiness, and bliss.

But if anger overwhelms you, in that case, you will end up destructing your inner self, your surroundings, and everything you touch, so learning how to soothe down this internal force, and direct it in constructive directions, is going to be a crucial point in finding and creating inner harmony and stability.

A fire within me was urging me to break through; in that specific moment, I was in awe of its power, its fearlessness, and its rebellion, but I foresaw the scene where I was completely burned down, alive, by a part of me, that I took pride in, it took a hold of me, in such a way, that I couldn't understand nor explain, it filled me up, only to proceed with the act of destroying me, I asked myself, how can a part of you, be your worst enemy, a contradiction, a whole another nature, that presents itself in the most devious form, I couldn't find an answer, but I know for a fact, that I can be its destroyer too.
A human

Hate

Love is ingrained in the human psyche, and it is the ultimate objective we all strive for throughout our lives, the never-ending search for a pure form of connection that transcends the mundane, palpable, and mortal nature of life itself, ecstasy, unity, and immortality, within what is graspable for the human awareness, but what happens when this feeling morphs into its polar opposite?

Hate is a pressing desire to destroy something, similar to a difficult-to-control or silent pulse. It is forceful and venomous.

The question that arises is what could be the probable cause for the presence of such feeling, what causes this complete shift in nature from sublime purity to ultimate depravity.

Many ideas come to mind: does the presence of polarity in everything imposes having this emotion as part of the human experience? Is it a strange form of attachment that contains much repulsiveness? Or is it a normal reaction to what is different and unknown?

Each idea could be taken and dissected so that it makes sense in its unique way, but what is essential is that this feeling is profoundly present in our world, in every way conceivable, towards different ideologies, organisations, and people, and the consequences of it have manifested themselves in the various conflicts and struggles that are dominating our day and age. Furthermore, because the nature of this emotion is very covert and dark, it tends to lurk beneath the surface, growing slowly and potently until it reaches the point of taking over one's general nature, a nature that conspires in a devious manner to find satisfaction through the demolition of its provoker, which leads to what we see daily of hate crimes and attacks that inexplicably disturb us, because our pure nature values life in all of its forms, we find it difficult to accept that a fellow human could be capable of such callous and wicked crimes.

Hate has a devious nature. It consists of utter dislike, combined with disgust and sometimes even anger; it's bitter and spiteful towards the source of the emotion. However, what's interesting is that it's a reaction towards specific situations, individuals, and even beliefs and ideas.

As the emotion develops towards these aspects, an inner viciousness emerges, putting the individual into a highly negative internal state. Although the wish here is to have all of the experienced emotions reflect on the other individual, the individual himself is still the one who is affected by them, which brings up a critical point to understand, and that is what you generate is what you become; it's what you can't separate yourself from because it's what creates and moulds your nature. So being continually filled and absorbed with a poisonous feeling like hatred is going to harm your inner self and everything you touch, which is why it's the polar opposite of the divine nature we aspire to represent, a nature that extends, forgives and loves unconditionally.

Learning how to cleanse your heart from this emotion will be life-changing. As you let go of the shadow aspects that are muddled and poisoning your soul in many ways, most of which are probably unrealised and unacknowledged, you will begin to rise above all of the darkness that you have filtered the world through, and a free, saintly version of you will emerge who only knows how to see the world through the eyes of love and compassion.

Causations

Pre-Existing Biases

We are made up of many events that shape us physically, mentally, and emotionally, as by nature, we are affected by everything that we come across, whether that is something that is realised or not, however, the consequences of these external forces are different in nature, with some having a beneficial and consistent impact on us. In contrast, others might lead to our devastation and ruin.

The aspects that determine our emotional reaction to the external world, such as what we like, dislike, desire, and avoid, are deeply rooted and require much digging and inspection to find the reasoning behind them; analysing along with a heightened sense of awareness is essentially what is going to allow us to unravel the deep complexities that reside in our psyche, particularly when it comes to emotion as poisonous and wicked as hate, as it may result in several catastrophic outcomes for the inner self, interpersonal relationships, and social life.

Planting seeds: Childhood is the most fascinating stage of life because it is the stage of exploration. Children's eyes are unclouded by preconceived notions or prejudices; their nature pushes them to observe and understand.

The child's need to explore his surroundings is what leads those around him to care for him, and this care may sometimes be a definite conductor of feelings of hatred because they ultimately have the most significant influence on the child's personality and view of the world.

They shape and mould his internal being according to the model that they present, and a child is essentially like a sponge; he absorbs the many actions, reactions, and even subtle gestures that the caregiver displays and the environment that he provides is what creates what is acceptable, what is frowned upon, and what is hated and despised for the child.

The development of the child's awareness allows him to begin to create associations between the caregiver's teachings and biases with the various human emotions, some are positive, while others are negative, so any extreme behaviour displayed by the caregivers will cause the child to experience an intense emotional response.

What can be particularly dangerous is for the caregivers to display any form of careless, humiliating, or hurtful behaviour towards the child because, in the child's eyes, the caregiver is the saviour and protector; receiving this sort of treatment from the person viewed as the safety net will provoke many negative emotions, that will be imprinted within the realms of his unconscious, and severely pierce through his psyche.

Displaying the emotion of hatred in front of a child is destructive to his emotional development; even if it is not aimed against the child himself, the proclamation alone is enough to arouse and infect the child with such emotion; because let's not forget that children are very much like sponges and tend to mimic and copy all the behaviours of the adults around them to understand and make sense of the world.

The compass: Early learning to see the world through hate-filled eyes will be highly destructive because it establishes the lens for one's perception, a perception that is filled with hate and enmity towards any differences that the outside world presents; it will destroy one's ability to build a proper moral standard based on the love of good for everyone unless one makes the conscious decision later in life to separate himself from what he has been taught and infected with and choose to awaken the love that is contained in every human soul.

What affects a child's structure is the expansion of his social circle, or his environment, which is equally powerful in inciting feelings of hatred because those close to him are also impacted by their social and cultural environments and reflect these influences in their interactions with the child.

Drawing the lines: Adolescence marks the beginning of the stage of self-identification, which allows the person to know himself and decide what he desires; however, both of these periods are characterised by a complete absence of inner clarity and stability because these two qualities can only be attained by experience and understanding. Therefore, a person's high receptivity during these life stages, coupled with a lack of these two crucial components, necessitates that they are significantly impacted by all unpleasant and adverse outside events and circumstances, which can be extremely crippling and destructive to the person's capacity for self-regulation.

Family environments that are filled with hate produce hateful individuals with psychopathic tendencies, even if the hate acts were not directed at the individual himself, because we humans, by nature, cannot help but be infected with the emotions of others, so if an individual resides in an environment that constantly displays acts of violence and hatred, especially in the early stages of his life, this will affect him to grow up and become filled with emotions of hatred and vengeance, and if one didn't recognise his hate-filled nature and its dangers to others he will end up falling a victim for emotions of hate.

The social environment is as powerful in moulding and influencing our emotional responses. Try to think about your social circle and what it represents for you. If you think about it enough, you'll realise that it's an excellent representation of the world you live in. The social environment determines whether we are accepted or rejected, which can be encouraging or discouraging. These two aspects significantly affect our emotional states and the nature of our life journey. Individuals who are excluded from their social environment because of their notable differences from their peers suffer greatly because being rejected and excluded often brings about a sense of unworthiness that evokes a wide range of negative emotions that lead to hatred.

We find this to be very prevalent among groups of minorities who are completely vetoed out of their society, such situation is extremely painful because it is elicited by a general feeling of rejection in the air, it is haunting and daunting, and it takes a hold of one's inner state in such a suffocating and unavoidable way, this high form of pressure and unease due to not being accepted nor appreciated is highly detrimental to all forms of positive emotions, and it leads to extreme levels of hatred towards the rejecting group, and this specific circumstance may have many other expressions, of either driving the individual to a downfall to depression, or being utterly angered and hateful and showing these feelings by seeking to cause ruin and damage, which will end in greatest disasters and devastation, both of these situations highlight the necessity of living among a society that is accepting and welcoming to one's originality and individuality, for the reverse can result in a life of misery.

Don't create your enemy: The cultural environment must be the most interesting since, after all, what is culture? It's the traits and knowledge of a particular group, including language, religion, social customs and values, and much more.

These traits unite various groups of people and set them apart. Still, occasionally these held sets of values can be the cause of certain negative emotions, as an excessive amount of fanaticism for these shared traits will result in a hostile and hateful reaction towards anything different or new, for many people feel a sense of grandeur and power in what they have in common with this large group.

Cultural teachings may also suggest hatred for other beliefs and behaviours.

This is something that has persisted throughout human history; there has always been a conflict between groups with conflicting values, and when we investigate it from a more individualistic perspective, we discover that each person's cultural background significantly affects their likes and dislikes on a neutral exterior scale of things, as well as what they love and hate on a deeper level.

To give an example, certain cultures that possess more liberal values in contrast to the more conservative ones, the people who belong to the first group will have an incomprehensible and disgusted reaction to the conservative values, while conservatives will view the liberals in an overly harsh and immoral way, Both of them are on opposing ends of the political spectrum, which implies a significant gap separating the two parties in a very distinct way.

They both symbolise two separate worlds that cannot cross paths or interact in any way, creating an aura of foreignness that requires from each party a much-needed defence, and oftentimes, this defence consists of hatred, you may wonder why, because hate is an emotion that is based on the desire to completely destroy what it has attached itself to, and when it comes to what provides one with a sense of security and power, there is a tremendous sense of attachment to it to an almost sacrificial extent, where one will do anything to establish and protect what he believes in, and psychologically it is shaped as the utmost desire of ruin for its rival. It's a defence mechanism that provides a sense of safety for those who choose not to conform to their beloved set of ideals; as a result, many people develop rigidity and rejection towards others who come from different cultural backgrounds, mocking their traditions and disrespecting their different values; it's a phenomenon that exists in every corner of this world, and it requires much-needed re-evaluating and changing in order to find much-needed peace and acceptance in the world.

Finally, past experiences undeniably influence our emotional reactions because every situation unconsciously impacts us in different ways and on different levels; some are more subtle, while others create focal points in our lives that result in great transformation.

In general, the intensity of a situation is determined by how impactful it is emotionally, so when one goes through a situation that enlivens fiery feelings of abhorrence, momentarily, the emotion is potent and debilitating to an extreme extent. Still, over time, these emotions are soothed and regulated. Still, a lingering after-effect remains; a haunting shadow of the past event lives within one's psyche, resulting in an attempt to find certain associations with the event and the experienced emotions, which will eventually create biases that may evoke the same feeling towards different people, objects, or events.

For example, if one was wearing a black shirt during an occurrence that he considers to be the worst event of his life, he may come to loathe the colour black and link it with bad luck. If you met someone and terrible things began to pile on you, you may start to despise this person and associate the individual with all the horrible things going on in your life; because the human mind is always on a mission to recognise patterns and make associations and it's an essential aspect of how we make sense of the world, However, seeing the world through the lens of the past is a manipulation of perception; what is already known is part of the merged general knowledge that one acquires over the course of his life, it enables insight into possibilities, but it does not represent the present moment, and its possible causes and effects. So one constantly needs to purify his perception, for one cannot gain clarity with the residues of what has passed, though, for some, this type of emotional association can come about as mere intuition, where an unexplained negative emotional reaction occurs from the moment that one meets the triggering object. To try to explain this is a rather complex mission, as it's true that some people have a more insightful nature that can sense and predict future events, but another way to perceive this situation is with the idea that associations create patterns that produce a continuous cycle that starts with the first created link up since we all realise the power of each formed idea. It's the creator of every action that manifests physical reality, and anticipating an occurrence that generates spiteful feelings will undoubtedly bring it to existence!

Fear of Oneself

Have you ever tried to shed light on the parts of yourself that you suppress? The ones that you only act out when no one is looking, the parts that you keep hidden and in the dark, your everlasting secret, or have you treated them as if they don't exist, as if they don't stand in the corner of that dark chamber that represents a large part of your truth, the truth of who you are?

One's identity and character are typically prone to change; one life-changing incident might result in a complete shift in perspective, resulting in a general change in character; nevertheless, these kinds of shifts don't appear to occur frequently as each of us yearns to reach a point of identity establishment, followed by a strong rigidity established around one's views and beliefs. However, this is a minor step in a long process that includes many inspections and searching for what makes one desirable and loved and what can lead to rejection and loneliness.

These observations generally begin at a very young age, as a child is constantly urged to have his desires satisfied by the adults around him. To achieve this fulfilment, a child must develop an attitude that serves this need, according to the adults around him, since they are the ones that establish these kinds of standards, a pattern begins to emerge between actions and behaviours that lead to rewards and those that lead to punishment or denial of wants.

These associations expand and multiply with age, contributing to one's personality evolution and development, you may question how we all have this urgent need to be liked and appreciated; this need tends to control our conduct, but the one who sets what is desirable and likeable is the outside world. This forces us to display just specific traits and behaviours while erasing the other aspects of ourselves that are typically seen negatively. This leads us to experience an inner split and conflict as if we must remain in a constant state of hiding, pushing and tugging between our conscious awareness and our unconscious working mind, now the question that is arising inside you is how can this result in emotions of hatred.

The first stage begins with the repression of certain elements of one's self; it happens through the observation that they may result in exclusion or rejection, and as the individual continues to exhibit more and more of the desired and praised behaviour, a sense of contentment and self-confidence prevails as the individual begins to remove any risks of being rejected by the outside world, though the internalised existence of the other not desired aspects remains there, lingering and resulting in a form of inner contradiction, which results in one pushing these aspects of himself that he rejects into the unconscious realms of his mind, leading them to be more concreted on a level that he is unaware of. However, this lack of awareness doesn't mean that they don't affect nor impact him, but rather control his identity operation in ways that he doesn't seem to grasp nor understand, and they manifest themselves in many harmful feelings and actions where these elements that were deemed unwanted or undesired are projected onto others in an effort to escape the difficulty that comes with recognising and repairing these characteristics. Because it's easier for one to distance himself from what can make him unlovable than it is to confront the repercussions of revealing it.

For example, if you find yourself hating someone for being outspoken and social, even though these are two positive qualities, you still find yourself extremely spiteful towards the person who possesses them. Notice how these two characteristics that you identified the person with are what triggered your hateful emotions; think of it this way: if you are comfortable and accepting of yourself, why would someone else's character trigger you so much? Perhaps you have heard comments along the lines of 'you are too much', 'you need to calm down', or 'your high energy is troubling people', and this has led you to believe that being outgoing and social is negative or undesirable.

Such emotional reaction and involvement demonstrate that one can project parts of himself that he hates onto others in an attempt to cope with them; even if it ends up misleading and distorting his perception. It's still easier to consciously hate someone than to hate a part of yourself, in a way it's connected to the survival instinct that motivates us all to establish and protect ourselves, escaping the deception in who we are to increase our chances of survival.

The fundamental issue that emerges is that this type of emotional operation is linked to the subconscious mind, which indicates one's lack of awareness of the reality of his inner self and its wounds, so it is critical to be able to recognise this pattern within yourself and to look at it without denial or judgement, as the first is essentially the root of enslavement to any negative aspect one may possess. The second is what prevents one from finding compassion within his heart for himself and others.

Repeated Cycles of Emotional Abuse

Good treatment and interactions with others are defined as a set of intentional behaviours and actions contributing to one's overall well-being. However, the definition of this concept is ambiguous because what is considered to be enriching is typically only understood within the context of each individual's experience; what's more intriguing is that we frequently experience being torn apart and destroyed by those we hold dearest to us, leaving us with the most horrifying anguish that sparks the emergence of the most virulent feeling of all: hatred.

The causes for this shift are often confusing. Is it because many people have a distorted view of what is good and evil and end up accidentally harming us, or because many people on this earth are absorbed by their misery and end up bleeding it out on others?

Both options are just as terrible and present, so it's critical to grasp the dynamics that lead to such a flip of emotions so you don't end up sliding down the rabbit hole of such negative emotional change.

Don't wear the mask: We must first grasp what a good relationship looks like. It begins with two people joining forces, focusing on expanding and concentrating their connection with the presence of respect, love, understanding, and compassion, integrating all of these qualities to attain perfect harmony. The absence of any of these elements would result in an imbalance and friction between the two individuals because it removes a critical component that is necessary for any human connection, and with the nature of life, problems and issues always seem to present themselves to us in many different forms, but the one that is most powerful and destructive is that related to our connections, as the level of intimacy and closeness dictates the need for vulnerability, which is fundamentally removing and stripping away all layers and means of protection that we may use. It means we have to show up raw, unfiltered, and completely vulnerable and engaged with others.

Connecting on this deep level is beautiful, and it's what most people desire throughout their lives; even though many may try to avoid it due to their fear of being hurt, It is still one of humanity's ultimate desires.

Our obsessions: Don't fool yourself by wearing a mask for protection; the frightening side is that being unprotected puts us in danger of being emotionally harmed and abused. The abuse usually starts with a disruption in the good flow of the connection, leading to an emotional explosion for one or both persons, the level of pain felt during such times is a significant determinant of how the fragmented parts will realign together, potentially creating either a similar dynamic that is more guarded or a completely different one that is dominated by all the negative emotions that were felt and experienced.

It is worth noting that in both of these situations, one's ability to trust, forgive, and sympathise is affected; because one cannot grasp the thought of being violently hurt by someone he has trusted and confided in. This shock will undoubtedly cause a reaction, and this reaction often consists of becoming more cautious, lessening the level of trust that previously existed, alongside the preoccupation with the experienced pain leading to a certain level of aloofness towards the other, in many situations. This reaction still allows room for forgiveness, if the individual is presented with changed behaviours that show true regret and remorse, but if not, the ability to forgive will drastically become less likely, leading to a horrible and hate-filled scenario between two people who were previously untied by love.

Don't imprison your mind: The interesting thing is that hate is related to attachment because it's what allows such battles to blow out of proportion and get exponentially worse. The fear that motivates such feelings is too powerful and restraining that it ends up debilitating the individual's ability to properly assess the situation. It runs on a much deeper level that one cannot help but surrender himself to it. It's what we see and witness in many relationships throughout our lives.

The contradiction in the transformation from the state of love to hate is always painful and perplexing. Still, when we dig deeper, we discover that it's the gradual loss of each individual's fundamental needs, accompanied by attachment, that paves the way for a never-ending cycle of hurt and destruction; it is critical to understand how your attachment may be your captivity. It is what holds you down and corners you within your negative emotions and thoughts, yet it is exhilarating to realise that you can free yourself from these pain-inflicting dynamics.

Humiliation

In a world founded on competition that is formed from the notion of wins and losses, we find ourselves in an illusionary war between our inner self and the outer world, continuously attempting to cross a finishing line that does not appear to exist. On this never-ending journey, each individual chooses his unique form of strategy to move ahead; some may keep a glaring eye that is solely focused on what's ahead. In contrast, others may select the obstruction of others as an outmanoeuvre, the second option can take many shapes and forms, but the one that is the most harmful and destructive to others is humiliation.

Consciously choosing to humiliate someone to strip them of their pride cannot be a well-intentioned act. It's cruel and mortifying, however, is it an assertion of authority, letting the other know that they are inferior, or a type of punishment in aiming to inflict terrible pain on the other by destroying his pride and dignity.

There are many more possibilities to be made, but all we know is that experiencing humiliation is detrimental to one's emotional and mental welfare, and it can either lead to depression or becoming outraged and imbued with venomous hate. As a result, it's critical to grasp the true motivations behind such acts and how to cope with their emotional consequences.

To begin, what is pride? It is simply the sense of satisfaction inside oneself pertaining to one's successes or good actions; it's a type of positive emotional reaction that is vital and required for every individual's well-being, but what happens when someone attempts to ruthlessly destroy, and demolish this feeling using the most vicious means, to try and infuriate someone, denigrating their identity, accomplishment, and character are all tactics that might be used to instil emotions of unworthiness, humiliation, and inferiority in someone, and they can either be clearly directed or more passively displayed. In both cases, the receiving individual cannot help but be harmed when faced with behaviours with such intentions, as for the individual, all of these aspects are the parts that construct the structure that is called self, happiness and pride are derived and found within them. So a war ensues, between one attempting to fight back in order to harbour and protect these aspects, while the other uses every means possible to destroy them, however, this is not always the case, as those who lack the inner fortitude and self-defence mechanisms end up being completely crushed and destroyed, losing all of their self-esteem and inner strength to face the outside world, and possibly even descending into depression and making attempts at self-harm.

These critical situations typically occur to those who base their entire sense of inner well-being on the external validation of who they are and what they present; for those people, satisfaction comes not from their good deeds and actions but from how the world perceives them.

This way of associating external validation with emotional well-being is bound to cause an enormous amount of destruction, which comes not only from outside forces but from the inner self, which cannot be happy or content without this illusory stamp of approval; and even in mildly uncomfortable situations, the fragility of such sources of happiness will cause plenty of internal conflicts, but when faced with such cruel behaviour, the effects will destroy one's positive feelings.

Contrary to the brokenness that permeates this situation, a person with inner strength will undoubtedly be constrained by negative emotions, but differently, one that is fired, prepared to retaliate, and destroy his adversary.

This is where hatred commences in one heart because one's inner strength and desire to protect become strong enough to transform the feeling of hurt and pain into an eagerness to destroy the other. The feeling itself works as empowerment to attack and destroy whoever sought to crush the individual's identity; it gets attached to it in such a manner that it is determined to demolish, to remove the pain within and the threat that the other is presenting.

When you think about it, you will realise that hate is generally generated towards the experienced emotions of humiliation and belittlement, but because it is provoked by an external object, it becomes directed at it. When you meditate on this idea, you get to understand the pain of such emotion, which will allow you to justify it to some extent, but when you dig even deeper, you will uncover the truth which presents itself, and that is if an individual knows and understands the actual value of his existence, why would someone else's petty attempts to inflict pain and hurt evoke such feelings? It is only when you genuinely establish that your existence does not require any form of validation that you will be able to liberate yourself from the idea that someone can decide to set for you who you are in this world. You begin to see the truth inside the fact that there is no below or above, that everything is present and equal, and that this is part of the universal truth that doesn't require either validation or verification from anyone, and as you are part of this truth, you begin to realise that such attempts centre around the individual himself, his insecurities and inner turmoil.

Attachment

Reflect on the things you are connected to, what they are, and their role in your life. If you reflect sufficiently, you will discover that all of the things you are attached to in this life are nonphysical and ethereal, though they represent deep elements of yourself that maintain your desire to continue with life; however, could it be possible that our attachment to an individual, an outcome, the past, or a specific structure of things be the root cause of the majority of our suffering?

When we think of love, we often think of the many positive elements that go into its creation, such as affection, compassion, sympathy, and joy. The positivity within all of these emotions transforms their experience from just being lovely sentiments to a new state of being. The state of love, however, what could potentially change the nature of these emotions and flip them to their opposite side of unpleasantness, pain, and hate. When we look deeply into it, we discover that once attachment enters and dominates such a state, it ultimately sabotages its pleasantness and revokes its liberty.

Live the moment: For instance, consider a time when you felt a powerful sense of pleasantness with your lover; at the time, you were fully immersed and involved; your dreams were filled with anticipation for tomorrow, enjoying the moment with no worries and the splendour of love. Suddenly, however, an idea jumped into your head, and you gave yourself up for contemplation, and it was focused on the destruction and loss of that moment; she caressed your hand and brought your awareness back, but you were enslaved by the idea that one day she would leave you, and you focused on the meaning and permanence of the moment, and the fear of losing the moment took over you; you became wholly occupied by how to hold on to this feeling instead of experiencing it. This is the element of attachment demolishing the felicitous nature of love, replacing it with fear and anxiety.

I ring the bell for you: Be careful: The time for transformation has come, and you are the one who creates the enemy of fear, sadness, and anger, the catalyst for the massive explosion that causes hatred. You used the moment of love as a springboard for hatred and subconsciously reinforced it to use it as a conduit for your subsequent actions.

The secret to attachment lies in how we see individuals in our immediate environment, how much we value possession, and how much we value loss. Keeping the beloved in the circle of contentment and voluntariness signifies safety and continuity as an essential component of something the beloved has owned and will not accept to lose. Losing it would result in calamity, revolution, anger, and hatred if the beloved ends the relationship and shatters all the dreams painted for him.

What happens to you is that you cling to everything that gives you a sense of security, calm, satisfaction, and acceptance. You treat it as a vital component of you and refuse to accept its loss because loss equates to lose and rejection for you. The secret to attachment lies in your subconscious mind, which imposes limitations that would otherwise result in barriers and obstacles that are outward manifestations of love.

The attachment that was formed with the emotion derived from the object or expectation creates hostility around any change or outcome of an opposite nature. Still, when we genuinely try to understand such a dilemma, we find that the root cause for it is the reliance on these aspects for one's inner happiness and pleasantness, accompanied by fear formed around their absence or change. This sets up all the necessary elements to transform the state of love to its opposite, hate, the fixation with one's ideas of how things and people should be, creates spitefulness towards anything different. This is a form of internalised ignorance towards the truth of how mutable and changeable things are, and that relying on specific structures of things will only lead to pain, hurt, and misery. Once an individual learns how to detach himself from any predetermined conclusions, and then proceed to destroy them, he will come to understand the liberty that resides within each experienced moment.

Limitations and Constraints

Our freedom to pursue our desires and goals can frequently be restrained and shackled by various outside forces and interventions. This scenario can either be a short issue or an ongoing battle in our lives; however, the time component of such an issue significantly dictates its emotional ramifications.

For example, a momentary limitation will result in rage towards the imposing restriction object, but when such deprivation becomes a life-long struggle, it gradually plants the seed of resentment and hatred within the individual's heart. Being constantly stopped, cornered, and denied of what brings personal satisfaction and joy not only deprives the individual of the ability to experience positive emotions but also transforms into spitefulness and bitterness that overtake the individual and his perception of himself and others.

An individual's willpower essentially determines how far he goes in life, in following his goals and dreams, and in finding the inner fortitude to conquer any barrier that could arise along the road since the nature of life generally forces us to encounter particular challenges and adversities, to test and improve our willpower to push through and keep moving to progress on our path. However, there are times when a person's willpower wanes and weakens as a result of his inability to remove specific blockages.

This is bound to have emotional repercussions; initially, it may manifest as reactive sadness or anger towards whoever it is that caused the blockage, but when the problem persists and turns into a constant struggle, it drains the person's mental state by either being engulfed by despair and misery or by hatred for the limiting object or person. An individual who has consistently been denied their desires gradually begins to acquire a bitter attitude towards himself or others, depending on whether he views himself as the creator or the victim of his life.

An individual with a victim mentality would detest life and consider it as unfair and unjust, looking at it with a negative viewpoint, and even misplace the hate on others who seem to possess whatever it is that he is deprived of, whereas someone who holds themselves accountable is more likely to direct this spitefulness at themselves; self-hatred and flagellation become a habit that ends up destroying any positive emotions one might have.

One begins to feel ashamed and unworthy as he perceives himself as a failure. However, the interesting thing is that even in such a situation, the ingrained feelings of hate will undoubtedly affect others that exist within the individual's surroundings, as one's inner state always permeates through his actions and behaviours, regardless of the attempts to separate the two, they are two coherent aspects of a person that feed and set each other.

Pleasurable feelings lead to positive actions, and vice versa, so we find that even in situations where one's negative emotions are directed at oneself, they are bound to negatively affect one's connections and relations with others.

When a limitation is imposed by an individual, such as an authority figure or a close one, feelings of hatred will undoubtedly be directed at him. Still, generally speaking, one does not reach such a state of spitefulness and hatred until such restraint has persisted long enough, resulting in a life of depravity and misery; the situation here becomes dangerous as the feelings of being powerless, miserable, and deprived are incomprehensible, and often lead the individual to have a strong desire for revenge.

Someone's abusing their power and depriving you of your fundamental right to make choices and actions awaken the animal part of a human, the part that fights for its means of survival. Hatred becomes the emotion that reminds the individual of his desires while looking directly at the one who robbed it; in one parallel line that imposes the need for an uprising, one that determines who gets to win and overtake the other; in a sense, feelings of hatred serve as motivation in this situation since they prevent depression and despair from occurring. However, while feelings of hatred accomplish their intended goal of motivating the person, they also corrode the person's inner self, obliterate his capacity for empathy, and induce an obsession with the object of hatred that cannot be ignored or fled from.

Outcomes

Loss of Sympathy and Compassion

Empathy as an attribute is fundamentally one of the most crucial elements of a healthy personality. It is the capacity to look beyond yourself, putting aside your usual preoccupation with your thoughts and feelings, and gaze at the other with the desire to understand and experience their sorrow and misfortune, essentially this is the most crucial aspect one can possess to develop a genuine and healthy relationship with others, since, without it, a person will not be able to appreciate and understand the nature of others' internal experiences and how those experiences affect their behaviours and emotions. However, if one constantly experiences negative emotions, he will eventually lose this capacity, leading him to become consumed with his own unpleasant and painful emotions. As he loses sight of the suffering of others, he loses a core part of his humanity.

What actually happens is that hatred rules over the individual and begins to change the makeup of his identity and character, specific characteristics begin to take the lead while others gradually fade away, creating a high level of restriction on all positive emotions and their expression, mainly affecting one's ability to understand any kind of suffering other than his own, as the consumption with negative emotion that initially ignited the hatred is too powerful, that one cannot escape nor ignore, this consumption creates a vision block that limits one's perception only to his inner world and what is going on in it. It instils a false sense of righteousness and power within the inner spitefulness, and as previously stated, we tend to reflect our inner world onto reality, as our thoughts and emotions translate the outside world to us, giving us indications of whether we are affected positively or negatively by surrounding forces, however, they most importantly determine our general nature.

The significance of this situation is that the already loathsome nature is exacerbated by how it controls the individual's reality, so what happens here is that the ability to sympathise becomes exponentially reduced by repeated hate-evoking events. One becomes wholly stuck and stagnant within his inner world, becoming increasingly obsessed with the object of hatred, and ultimately losing the ability to extend any form of compassionate attitude for others.

What is especially dangerous about such a state is that the inner blockage leads to internal isolation that is highly poisonous and deceptive; the inner sense of loneliness aggravates the negative inner state even more and creates an illusion of righteousness that justifies hate and vengeance, and the object of hatred is the root of all evil, and it is existentially threatening and must be destroyed.

An external intervention might be helpful in dispelling such falsified beliefs, but the issue is that the general nature of hate is powerful yet hidden, lurking beneath the surface of every expression and interaction that the individual proceeds to make, and it's generally more difficult to detect than other emotions that have more direct paraded expressions. The isolation that emotion creates, makes it almost impossible for the individual to escape its poisonousness, blinding the individual's vision of others and their emotions, and demolishing any ability to extend neither compassion nor sympathy, which eliminates any possibility of creating any form of healthy connection with others.

Own your key: It's a hazardous situation because, without the ability to view others as human beings with emotions and feelings, one begins to behave differently, in a way that disregards the importance of people and their existence. They are dehumanised, and their only value is whether they feed into one's demands or not, and the further one gets into such a state, the more difficult it is for him to rid his heart of this venomous emotion, but one must constantly remember that he holds the key to transformation and self-improvement inside himself.

Dominance of Wickedness

Evil resides in the human psyche and its savage primal drive to survive; and if we attempt to unravel the genuine source of evil, its generator, we may come across a plethora of alternatives; some may argue that the thirst for power is the root of evil, there is more debate about the origin of evil, but what is certain is that the ignorance can indeed allow the roots of evil to extend and spread their roots to the point of no return because when an individual's behaviours are not dictated by his awareness, he becomes an entity ruled by its urges and instincts rather than the never-ending knowledge of all that exists on this earth.

We've all been faced with evil at some point in our lives, and we've all reacted to it in our unique way; some surrendered their forces to it, while others fought it back with a force that is even more devious and destructive. The dilemma is that if we were faced with evil and chose to respond to it with the exact nature, are our actions justified, or do they reinforce the destructive streak that we all have in some way or another?

The truth is that a person who surrenders to the disparities in other people's natures will always experience a wide range of unfavourable emotions. This is because such an individual allows the outside world to affect his internal self; as a result, the individual essentially doesn't own himself, but rather the negativity that resides in the external world owns him.

When an individual allows the external world to instil in him feelings of hatred, he gradually loses all of the positive emotions he has previously experienced and instead becomes filled with feelings of envy, spitefulness, and vengefulness, that his perception becomes distorted in such a way that he draws the illusion that this world is all evil, and such distortion allows him to act deviously and find justifications for his actions. However, when we try to analyse the point of arrival to such a state, we find that every individual has the potential for the expansion of evil, some are more easily prone to it due to their early exposure to cruel and vicious environments and individuals, while others are less likely unless confronted with shockingly hostile and inimical situations or individuals. The difference between these two situations is that in the first, one must develop a strong will and orientation towards goodness in order to fully tame and control the potential for evil, whereas, in the second, it is a much easier road to simply follow the conscientiousness that one is familiar with. It is an inner battle between the most rooted aspects of a human, to choose whether to go down the path of wellness or the path of destruction, to intentionally pick which part of yourself to nurture and grow.

Painting a picture of how hatred can obliterate all good in a person is challenging because every state of hatred has distinct points and turns. Some people become fully consumed by the emotion and attached to it to the point where they are unable to control it, which causes them to feel a spike of need to express it.

However, each person's expression of hatred is different, so for some people, this expression may be hate speech and attacks on others, while for others, it may be full-blown hate crimes; for another group of people, it is more of a dark emotion that colours their inner self and psyche, but it is pressed and controlled in such a way that it destroys their inner self and desire to do good for others without it being fully expressed. Instead, envy, spite, and ill will towards others become their primary inner motives, two distinct but related circumstances in terms of the increase of evilness and the loss of traits that dignify a human, hatred, desire for demolition, and evil intents are the kinds of emotions and motives that turn one from being the unique being on this earth into utmost levels of evil. This existence lives on the annihilation of all that crosses its way.

Free yourself: The state of hate is an unfortunate state to be in because it imprisons and isolates you within walls of evil; however, one of your life's greatest missions is for you to see yourself in your true light, of good or bad, virtuous or evil, and to honestly admit to yourself where you stand within these polarities; only then, will you find your path to liberation, the liberation of anything or anyone that might control or imprison you.

Prejudice and a False Sense of Righteousness

What is right and what is wrong is a question that frequently crosses many minds; the minds of those who constantly question their actions in an attempt to perform acts of dignity and righteousness towards themselves and others, though unfortunately, this questionnaire finds its ending chapter, when many conclude that they have reached a point of fulfilment with their knowledge of justice and the righteousness of actions, forgetting that every stage, situation, and circumstance in life has its unique twists and turns that provide hints and clues of the right direction to take and the right actions to do and that whenever these signs are ignored due to one's delusional idea of complete knowledge, imprisonment occurs that is coloured with pure ignorance that leads to wrongful and harmful actions and reactions.

As stated earlier in the book, the emotional state tends to dictate many aspects of every individual's life, emotions hold far more importance than imaginable, and the more powerful and consumptive an emotion is, the more it defines and colours one's character and life as a whole, a poisonous emotion such as hate will undoubtedly have its effects just as any other consistently experienced sentiments. However, due to its demolition-oriented nature, its urges tend to be far more destructive and hurtful; though in order for these impulses to present themselves, justifications of the feelings and their manifestations must take place, either by hatred being a taught emotional reaction in previous years, or by one's own search for defects and dislikes in the target of hatred that support the pre-existing prejudice and offer a sense of righteousness to the emotion. The difficulty here is that the sense of right that one feels in his attitude is nothing more than an illusion, a self-created vision barrier that supports and feeds into one's current venomous inner state, giving it a sense of strength that, if acted upon, might lead to disasters.

Once these justifications are firmly established, one becomes blind to his inner toxicity and spitefulness as they get masked by the many rationales that one uses to enable himself to completely experience the unpleasant feeling, but what this does is that it forms an internal barrier, that distracts the individual from his inner toxicity. The essential issue is that the justifications provide room for increasing and empowering the emotions, while also diminishing the potential of self-analysis and introspection, one becomes entirely blinded by hatred to the point where he is unable to see, assess, or understand himself in the light of truth, it is a crippling state until one intentionally chooses to break through and change the way he sees himself and the world.

In essence, one's sense of righteousness is what also makes room for prejudice; it's the instilled notion in a person's mind that his ideas, beliefs, and concepts resemble the ultimate truth, and anything different or opposite essentially contradicts these absolute facts; coupled with the emotional investment accompanied by close-mindedness and the inability to accept differences; this eventually results in premade negative conclusions about people who belong to certain groups. However, if we exclude the emotional aspects, we will discover that the conceptual differences will only result in long and tedious arguments, but the emotional investment infused with concluded biases is what leads to the rise of negative emotion, most likely either anger or hate.

Anger is the more immediate emotional reaction, while hate is the internalised aversion and enmity towards certain groups who resemble a hated ideology or belief. When we look closely, we find that the hate that leads to prejudice is often provoked by ideas or concepts rather than individuals themselves, but because they represent them, the hate ends up being directed at them directly.

This is an issue that is present beyond belief in the world that we live in today. We find and even cross paths with many individuals who hate different ideas, cultures, and beliefs simply because they create opposition or present a contradiction with what they believe in, viewing the world in such a way will eventually lead to a heightened sense of inner bitterness, which, while seemingly directed at others, ends up affecting the individual the most.

Constantly judging, concluding, and moralising or demoralising others will only result in a hazy vision of reality, where your emotions obstruct you from seeing things for what they truly are, misinterpreting your entire reality by the one faculty that is supposed to be your greatest gift.

One must learn to admit ignorance, as not knowing is the beginning point for knowledge. To lose all sense of righteousness will stabilise your emotional state and allow you to see the world with the eyes of an explorer who looks to see and learn without passing judgement and prejudice.

Solutions

Consciously Practice Compassion

Having a holistic perspective of the world enhances your capacity to see yourself in everything and everyone. This viewpoint also allows you to suspend your ego and fully experience the moment. Compassion is primarily the key element that opens the door for even the slightest taste of this sensation; it will be rewarding for every part of your life to learn how to become mindful of not just yourself but also your whole environment, comprehending and witnessing their hardships and tribulations as though they were your own. The self is what creates each individual's experience on this earth. It's your own uniquely articulated lens through which you see the world, but your greatest gift can also be your greatest curse, as we find that many people live their lives burdened by their emotions and thoughts, the solitude of the internal self becomes too chaotic and hazardous that one's life experience turns into a nightmare.

To emphasise the word 'solitude' and give it a more robust definition and meaning, we may define it as 'full absorption with the inner self', with negativity, either through self-pity or self-flagellation, it is similar to being stuck in a negative environment but more covert and harmful because the internal self is a place of complete isolation. It's your own world that no one can alter or change but you. This creates a challenging dynamic of the need to look both inward and outward equally, as one must comprehend his own inner workings and processes while also recognising outside interventions and their impacts, and when it comes to the process of learning compassion, one has to learn how to provide this attitude first to himself and then to others.

It is difficult to start the flow of giving inside both ends of the direction; therefore, it is best to start by giving yourself much-needed compassion. You may wonder how; there are several approaches, but the most successful is to be kind to yourself, your flaws, errors, and wrongdoings of the past; to forgive and embrace all of these seemingly terrible elements of yourself will allow a certain amount of relief to emerge, and you gradually but steadily begin to let go of much of the baggage from the past that is infesting your heart with hateful emotions.

You must understand that this is not an overnight process, and it will take time and effort for you to start sensing some real difference with your internal voice and how it's guiding you through situations and circumstances. You must also remember that frustration and stagnation are part of the process, as they are both your guides informing you of the need for patience and tenacity to go forward with your inner transformation.

Once you notice a real difference in how you deal with inner negativity, you are a little more sympathetic and less hard on yourself, and you will instantly and spontaneously see that your perception of others has slightly changed. You are not as harsh or critical as before, and this change broadly relates to the fact that you treat others in the same manner that you treat yourself, and as you begin to give yourself some compassion, it becomes a part of you that you can deliberately offer to others. However, a distinction must be made between self-pity and the victim perspective vs the compassionate self-view. The first is characterised by inner weakness and fragility that one cannot help but seek ways to escape the nightmare of responsibility, whereas, the second is a powerful stance that one takes in which he can assess his wrongdoings, acknowledge and accept them, and move forward more informed and enlightened to where he took the wrong steps and actions, to not repeat the same mistakes when we say be compassionate with yourself; we mean don't waste your life focusing on previous mistakes, but rather accept them as a necessary learning curve that teaches you your most valuable lessons.

Consider the ability to extend the attitude of compassion as a muscle that must be exercised and used frequently to grow stronger. To become a more compassionate human being, you must become conscious of the concept itself and repeatedly attempt to practice it in your day-to-day life. To do so, immerse yourself in your pain and focus on the pain itself; now, see how bad you feel and picture another individual in the same scenario; they will undoubtedly endure the same suffering you endured, right?

Internalising this straightforward idea will enable you to put yourself in others' shoes, experience their sorrow, and afterwards let go of judgements and conclusions; in a sense, you elevate your humanity to a level that enables you to transcend above the ordinary and selfish nature that we all occasionally possess.

The unity that compassion develops in one's heart is so strong that it drives out the most hateful and wicked emotions of all. After all, hatred is fundamentally an emotion that is demolition-oriented, wanting you to entirely demolish the object of hate, and this is accomplished in part by dehumanising the object itself, which is the polar opposite of compassion.

Consider it this way: You have an inside pressing desire to destroy something, based on your feeling of righteousness, along with inner agony and dehumanisation of the despised object; all of these distinct parts combine to form a tremendous force that allows the emotion to expand and dramatize itself. However, if we try to introduce the component of compassion into the scene, we will notice that it will gradually but steadily begin to deconstruct the different elements that allow room for growth for the feeling, as it is primarily the compass that signals you to see the same human qualities that you feel yourself in others, and this change of perspective will also lead to changes in your sense of what is right and wrong, which will allow you to drop the uprightness that you feel, step by step, as you begin to consciously practice different ways of providing compassion to yourself and others. You will find that you are no longer hateful or spiteful, your inner state is much more harmonious and pleasant, and you are able to truly involve yourself in your surroundings, leaving behind the constant self-absorption that is leading you to so much misery and pain.

After discussing all of these different concepts about compassion and how to practice it, it is critical to remember that 'compassion' does not imply drowning yourself in other people's issues and misfortunes; it is an essential tool for connecting with others, but it can also be a two-edged sword. This is especially true for those who are born with the quality of compassion, where they find themselves burdened and overweight with others' suffering due to their hypersensitivity to emotions and suffering, you must never forget it is of utmost importance to practice your humanity in its highest form that centres on unity and oneness. Still, you must also learn how to draw a necessary line between your inner self and the outside miseries and mishaps.

Opening Perception

We live in a diverse world where many different cultures, religions, and customs exist. For each person, these differences can either be uncharted territory that piques their curiosity or a dangerous area that threatens them.

When we stop to think about it, we discover that how we choose to approach the uncharted and unknown areas of life has a significant impact on our inner self and its state for those who are willing to accept and delve into what is categorised as foreign tend to be much happier and pleasant, in contrast to those who are too rigid and confined within their little world.

The idea resides that once acceptance is learned and mastered, a person becomes an explorer who views every challenge, obstacle, and even opposition as an opportunity to broaden his knowledge and perspectives rather than as a catalyst for his ingrained resentment and spite.

As explained earlier in this chapter, even though hate is primarily internal, it has a robust illusionary fog that makes it appear to be about the other, while in reality, it is focused on one's deepest wounds and traumas. This illusion creates an appearance of righteousness that allows the emotion to persist and grow, and to clear this fog and remove it; one must become aware of this truth; the process of raising awareness involves confronting oneself and changing one's perspective.

To start, one must accept and understand that the external trigger only serves as a pointer to a deep, unresolved, and rejected part of oneself. This will cause the focus to shift from the external trigger to your internal self, which is essentially where the emotion resides, although this might seem like a simple task to complete, it is not because when the feeling consumes you, it places limitations on your vision and acceptance. Therefore, one needs to muster enough humility and courage to reach such a point for this step to be established.

This is why it is called self-confrontation because you see yourself raw and unfiltered, which can be upsetting and painful, but it will surely bring you to the realisation that you need to make the change.

As you confront yourself, many truths about your internal state, your surroundings, and the root cause of your hateful nature will begin to reveal themselves to you. As painful as these realisations are, they are essential in the process of progressing through your self-improvement journey, and as you come to see that your spitefulness is entirely your responsibility, you begin to hold yourself accountable, paving the road for you to modify your viewpoint of yourself and others.

You may wonder how changing perception can alleviate feelings of hatred. In essence, your perception of situations and people determines how you are emotionally affected by them, so when you consciously choose to broaden your perception by removing mental limits and shackles, you allow yourself to see things for what they indeed are without having your emotions intrude and abrupt your view of reality.

To illustrate, you begin to understand that your spiteful nature may be the result of witnessing hatred around you early in your life; this is the root cause, but it's a missing conclusion because when you think about it, you will find that the past has undoubtedly influenced your nature, but the way you are today is primarily determined by whether you chose to break free from past negativity or whether you submitted and remained under their influence. It's a mental shift from being a victim to becoming a vital force in your life, and you also realise that the hatred you witnessed previously in your life was centred on others' wounds rather than your own, allowing you to have some sympathy and compassion instead of anger or hate.

Developing your understanding to such an extent will empower you enough to be able to connect the dots in a correct manner, where you can take responsibility for your emotions, know the root of your suffering and what caused it without being spiteful or vengeful, and know where to draw the boundaries to end toxic patterns that are hurting your well-being.

You must recognise the importance of developing a broad perspective of yourself, others, and the world; learning how to understand, accept, and process inner pain and suffering is your only path towards internal pleasantness; mapping out your emotions and their root cause is what will allow you to become conscious of your internal operations, and you become aware that outside forces are triggers and stimulants that push and guide you towards inner discovery to achieve serenity and happiness.

Gratitude

Gratitude is the quality of thankfulness and acceptance for what is received; it is a form of liberation because by being grateful for what crosses your path, regardless of whether it is negative or positive, your perspective changes, and you learn how to see the bright side of everything, which allows room for the elimination of many negative emotions, particularly hate, which is the most destructive and venomous.

When we try to analyse hate, we discover that a large part of its invasion stems from the root of non-acceptance, which is essentially you rejecting something so powerfully that you become entirely occupied by dismissing it, and you are unable to let go or detach yourself from it, though when we try to find methods and ways to soothe it down and eliminate it, we discover that the practice of specific emotional and mental habits can help exponentially. This is where gratitude comes in because a grateful person cannot despise or hate; he accepts everything with thankfulness, and this attitude minimises a large part of the negative emotional reaction one might have towards unpleasant situations, circumstances, or individuals, which is the main goal that one wants to accomplish in the process of destroying emotions of hate. We want to destroy the different components that construct the feeling itself, and through gratitude, one's core character undergoes a level of transformation, a flip from being hateful and outraged to becoming a more accepting and optimistic individual.

Gratefulness is not directly related to hatred, but it is a component that will awaken the humane aspect inside you; it's you battling against the emotion that is associated with evil and destruction by nurturing the elements within you that are opposite, it's like a war between two competing parts within every human, the more you work on and nurture one, the more powerful and dominant it gets, and when you sow the seed of gratitude in your heart, you have the strength to confront anything, you become aware that everything that crosses your path serves a purpose for your growth and expansion, and this understanding alone is powerful enough to stop you from hating and despising certain people or situations. You recognise that the most painful and triggering incidents in your life occurred for a reason, and not by chance, to guide you towards different parts of your internal self that need to be addressed and healed.

Developing Communication

Success, accomplishment, and goal-achieving largely depend on one's capacity for self-expression, a combination of the capacity for effective communication of ideas and concepts and the attractive presentation of talents and gifts.

A deficiency in any of these areas will result in specific roadblocks and difficulties in one's life, which will undoubtedly arouse many negative emotions, especially hatred because someone who is repeatedly misunderstood and underestimated will eventually come to hate both himself and the rest of the world. Therefore, learning how to better articulate and communicate will undoubtedly benefit your inner well-being.

Being able to articulate yourself clearly and effectively is a skill you must develop throughout your life. It will demand a lot of focus and attention from you, and you will undoubtedly encounter many obstacles along the way. However, remaining persistent and disciplined on this path is the most crucial thing.

You first start your journey by realising that for you to be able to articulate yourself clearly and effectively. You must have a thorough understanding of your internal operations, for they are what govern and control what you convey to the outer world, a person who doesn't understand himself properly will constantly find himself imprisoned within the tangles and kinks of his inner self and even including others in his complexities. Thus for you to avoid this trap, you must increase your self-awareness so that you are hyper-aware of how the outside world affects you. By becoming hyper-aware of these effects, you can address irritants and triggers as soon as they arise rather than allowing them to fester for extended periods, which is essentially the main reason why so many different negative emotions can turn into hate; for the repeated experience of pain can often turn into the desire to destroy of either one's self or others. This is a place you don't want to reach since it's a lot more difficult stage to overcome; you become obsessed with the illusion of hatred and misery to the point where you lose your grasp on reality. It's an exceedingly poisonous and terrible condition that you must do everything you can to avoid.

If you've read this far, you must now have a level of emotional understanding and intelligence; you can assess and analyse the basic human emotions and their triggers; and this understanding will allow you to better recognise the turmoil of your inner self, even though emotions are complex by nature, having a general sense of what could potentially trigger one emotion or the other will allow you to explore the depth and complexity of your sentiments on your own. Through this process, you will undoubtedly be able to better communicate yourself, and your awareness level will rise to the point where you will be liberated from the prison of impulses that are the result of negative emotions, although this is not a remedy to your hateful nature, it is a means to live life more delightfully, which is the only antidote to all negative human feelings.

You must recognise that your inability to adequately express yourself can sometimes be your greatest curse in life, and it can be the cause of many misfortunes and mishaps that you may face. However, this does not negate the fact that throughout your life, you may encounter individuals who are not in a good state internally, and they may inflict pain on you. These two facts exist equally, but holding yourself accountable in areas where you may be lacking will be your greatest gift to yourself, and you must embrace this fact with ease and comfort, as it is your doorway to self-improvement and progress.

Conclusion

Through this path of seeking to investigate and comprehend feelings of hatred, we've come to discover that it leans more towards being a type of orientation than it is merely an emotion; it's a dark, devious, and hidden nature, but when we think about it, we realise that no one was truly born hateful, but instead, either particular individuals or circumstances affected someone adversely to the extent that they polluted their nature in such a wicked way, which is extremely unfortunate.

When we try to think about why hate exists on a more individualistic level, we find that it's one of the significant tests that exist in each and everyone's life because it is a question of which path you will take: the path of growth, nurture, and expansion, or the path of destruction and ruin, which seed within you are you going to grow? This way of thinking shifts the focus to the idea that you have a choice in battling a part of you that has the potential to become evil and that you can try to cultivate a pleasant, good-loving nature.

It is not a matter of what will happen in the end; instead, it is a matter of what you decide to make of yourself. This is a solid position to be in because it means that you are in control of your destiny and all of its manifestations.

I fought, and battled with myself, my existence, and its potential. Why couldn't it just guide me? Why did I have to fight with a part of me I cannot detach from? Is it a matter of life and death, or does power bring destruction? In either case, I know that I can only find my liberation by flourishing myself and everything I get to touch!

A human

The Self-Reconciliation Process

Don't we all yearn to go back to point zero; the point in which we felt most free and open to experiences and life itself, unburdened by the mishaps of the past or worries of the future, the time when we felt most alive when we possessed the unfettered spirit of a child who doesn't know how to judge or conclude but only looks to see since we all seem to have grown to become miserable, confined, and limited by responsibilities, past experiences, and the realisation of our mortality and as a result of all of these factors, we became so absorbed with what the outside world imposes on us that we lost our genuine voice, our inner sensation that takes us towards the light, the light of our destiny, potential, and bliss?

We all go through life with an inherent sense of restriction that destroys the way in which we experience life. We can blame this sense on the many externally imposed restrictions that the outside world presents to us, but when we look deeply into ourselves, we discover many deep-rooted internal limitations that obstruct our pursuit of happiness and bliss. While we may mistake these limitations for our fundamental nature, they are, in fact, exterior layers and voices that we took on along our life path and have misidentified as our truth; the question that arises is how we can peel away all of these layers and rediscover our inner self, who only understands how to love, expand, and create a lifetime of bliss, happiness, and fulfilled purpose. The process must first be launched consciously. There must be an intention behind this process of self-reconciliation; as one must sincerely and totally wish to cleanse and reconcile with himself to be free to experience the magic of his being, the established intention essentially serves to set the direction for the process and steers the individual towards its ultimate goal, since without it, this would be an absurd process that leads nowhere, a transitory desire.

The main goal of this process is to remove all layers that aren't beneficial to your well-being and purpose in life, to let go of your fears, regrets, and guilt, and to give power to your higher self. Doing this will enable your innate wisdom and knowledge of everything to take over and direct you towards your purpose, people, and circumstances that will enhance and add to your life experience.

Align the Past with the Present Moment

Who you are at this very moment is a product of your life path, with all of its twists and turns, moments of success, failure, happiness, and suffering; these significant events in your life shaped who you are and moulded your nature to what it has become.

Now, go to a mirror and gaze deeply into yourself, not to analyse the shape of your eyes or the wrinkles on your face, but to glance deeply into your soul and all of its shattered pieces that haven't been fixed by time or the many places you've visited and the many people you've met.

Acknowledge the parts of you that you've tried to escape from one too many times, and reminisce about that moment when you've decided to hide from yourself, that moment when you allowed yourself to live with an illusion, not about anyone, but yourself, sit with this notion for a second, breathe it in, and allow it to occupy space within you; don't overthink or dissect it; instead, experience its existence in your body, and feel the sensation of finally acknowledging the truth that you've avoided for so long, look at your face and recognise all the negative emotions you have been experiencing for as long as you can remember.

Acknowledge that you have been living your life half-heartedly because you have constantly been afraid of failing, being rejected, being mocked, and of who you truly are; acknowledge that the power front you have been working so hard to maintain was only intended to shield you and mend your broken heart; accept that your anger was only a mask you used to hide your violent cry for love and compassion, admit that you've always felt weak and invisible and that the world hasn't yet shone its light on you, and that your childhood dream, after all, remained a dream, accept it all, breathe it in, and finally, admit that this is your truth.

Now is the time for you to analyse your lifeline and its major twists and turns, go down memory lane and recall all the significant moments of your life, right down from your childhood to your adult life, and write them down as if you were writing a story you want to tell the world, bring yourself, the scene, and others back to life, and relive all the moments along the way, relive the emotions, and how you came out of their experience, how different you've become, what you've lost and what you've gained, think in-depth about which elements of yourself you've left behind and which ones you've repressed, and watch your character develop.

Also, consider what others in the narrative represented for you, how much you gave them, and how much you took away; think in symbols and deeper meanings because others are merely representative of deep parts of yourself that you are unwilling to recognise; they are more than simply people; they are your mirror, which may sometimes be more true to you than yourself. Furthermore, don't judge; merely observe and accept because the minute you begin to judge, you become blind. Allow the tale to develop, and watch yourself become who you are at this very moment.

Observe the Present Moment

Now that you understand your life path and where it has led you, you must look around you, step outside of yourself for a brief moment, and observe who you are as if you were watching a stranger on the street from the corner of your window, don't add or subtract, simply observe how you've become, what you do, and how you reject the bliss that life offers you every day, observe how your dreams have faded, and how you've lost your way to love and that even though faces and places change, you still feel the same emptiness, the same void in you that you felt after your first loss and that you don't try anymore, you don't try to draw a smile on the faces of those close to you if anything, they have become a part of what you are used to, what you take for granted every single day of your life. Take a minute to watch yourself objectively and with curiosity rather than with judgment to ascertain who you genuinely are right now and how the many facets of your life have evolved. Look at how you treat what's important to you if you have any, and how you treat yourself. Do you show up every day for the person you know the most, the one you are most familiar with and whose difficulties and battles you are most aware of, the one you have neglected for so long? And how has your negligence affected others? Do you treat them as harshly as you treat yourself? Do you no longer notice them? Do they no longer exist for you?

Are they merely passing objects and noises to you?

At this stage, focus on two things: one, observing; you want to study yourself, your life, and others, you want to look to see how you treat everything around you, how much you give, and how much effort you put, how much you take and how much you accumulate, and two, you want to detect and work on losing your bias, you want to spot the mistake in your thinking that directs you towards what satisfies your beliefs even though it contradicts the truth, you want to stop generalising, justifying, and blaming. In essence, you want to alter your perception, the perspective that resulted in who you are and what your life is today; you want to become conscious of the things you were previously unable to perceive, the ones that caused you to misunderstand yourself, your life, and others.

Allow Space for the Real You to Emerge

We can now say that you are no longer lost, clueless, or confused; you have become aware of who you are at this very moment, of the whys, hows, and whens; you have shone a light on the deepest part of you that has been hidden for so long; and you have become the light. Take what you've learned and blow it away with the wind, let it free, and let it flow away into oblivion, allow yourself to feel free once again, to sense the light, the earth, and the beauty that was present from the beginning. Allow yourself to breathe the moment, allow your eyes to sparkle, and your soul to grin, enjoy every second of this glorious trip, and take risks, take chances on love, chances on adventures, and most importantly, chances on you, the person you should honour the most, the one who fought, struggled, and most importantly, kept you alive till this very minute, allow yourself to learn, explore, and feel what it means to be alive; forgive yourself and accept your imperfections; rediscover your passions and what makes you feel alive and let your creativity run wild, and most importantly, treat others in a way that respects what it truly means to be a human.

Now you want to direct your attention to the various areas of your life that need improvement, assess what's lacking, and devise a dynamic strategy to improve, make plans for your goals, and learn how to readjust along the way, make sure you show up every day for yourself by doing the things that make you feel good, and nurture your knowledge and skills, steer clear of the things that put you down and dampen your spirit, and make sure you hold yourself accountable for your actions, allow yourself to be touched by others and the magic of life itself; stay open and receptive to everything and everyone, and never let failure destroy your soul. Make a lifetime of happiness and delight for yourself, and remember to always be kind since kindness has the type of influence that lasts not only for a moment but for a lifetime. Now that you are free, fly on the horizon and enjoy the ride!

Doorways to Progression

Immersion

People who have achieved greatness in life have one thing in common: they all have the ability to access a high state of focus that is unaffected by daily life's burdens, personal fleeting thoughts and emotions, and their external environment. They understood that to create, they needed to leave themselves behind and become an instrument that serves their creation, and in doing so, they were able to play out their best performance and create remarkable things.

You must learn to become one with the object of focus, as this must be one of the most magical and satisfying states to be in; it is the essence of flow. However, to enter this state, you must first dissolve all barriers related to the (I) and fully immerse yourself in whatever it is that you are doing.

You may wonder how one can achieve this state, and the answer is that you must develop the ability to fully break through the mental blockage that often occurs as a result of the inability to shed the mental occupation with fleeting personal thoughts, and in doing so, you will be able to fully immerse yourself in the activity you are performing and, in a sense, become an extension of it, and that will allow you to access your total capacity of focus and, as a result, give your best performance, which will provide you with tremendous satisfaction, and to experience oneness with an object outside of yourself, your emotions, and your thoughts will allow you to experience a part of the liberation, the liberation that comes from not losing yourself but rather becoming a part of something bigger than yourself.

To enter this flow, you must first understand that you are constantly occupied with random thoughts and emotions, which are often unimportant but are nonetheless a part of your human nature. Once you have this understanding, you must begin to create a certain level of detachment from these thoughts and emotions, which allows you to be an observer rather than a slave to them, this will enable you to direct your pure and sharp focus in the right directions, and while this is not an easy process, it is achievable. You will need persistence, mental stability, and a strong desire to fully immerse yourself in something because without these qualities; you will not be able to narrow down your vision to become laser-sharp and focused.

In Denial Lies Weakness

Acceptance and rejection are two aspects that shape and form the direction of your life; what you choose to accept will have a powerful conscious influence on your decision-making and determine what you decide to pursue, whereas what you reject will remain present and equally influential, though it will reside in an unconscious and hidden realm, the realm where all of your deep-rooted desires and motives are created. Those two aspects combine to form who you are as a person, laying the groundwork for your reality and manifestations, being in denial about elements of yourself can only serve to hurt and detract from your growth and evolution.

Denying your desires, motives, and wounds will only allow them to expand and multiply over time, to the point where they become the controller and dictator of your outward expressions and actions, which in turn will have a direct effect on your emotional world and internal state. It's a cycle that connects one's innermost world with his reality, understanding this dynamic gives us a glimpse of the power of the unknown, that what is hidden holds immense power, and a large part of your mission in life is to dig deep within and unravel the depth and complexity of these hidden aspects of who you are, unlocking the power of your full potential and eliminating many unconsciously created trials and errors, and although it is difficult and painful to admit to yourself your flaws and imperfections, it is far more beneficial to confront them head-on, because by doing so, you become a true mirror to yourself, and instead of having others and the world reflect your complexities back to you, you become fully responsible for yourself and your internal state.

You will find that what you choose to reject within yourself will haunt you throughout your life, through situations, individuals, and even your actions. Learn to accept and embrace every part of yourself because in doing so, you shed light on the deepest part of your being, and in a sense, you become the light!

Self-Justifications

Every action has an equal reaction, which creates a dynamic of motion in life. This universal rule exists in what we see and what is beyond our humble capacity for observation. On a more individual scale, we constantly react to outside interventions and influences, which vary in nature, for sometimes they are of a positive and loving nature. Other times they stem from inner spite and anger, and whenever we find ourselves evoked in such a negative matter, which leads to acts of harm and destruction to others, we cannot help but seek justifications for our actions. However, the question that arises is whether these justifications serve a positive purpose, or whether they are a form of deception that reinforces one's inner desire to destroy.

When we honestly and sincerely try to meditate on this concept, we discover that justifications are a part of enslavement and a lack of personal responsibility. They imply that one cannot help but be influenced by the natures and inclinations of others, that they have the power and ability to awaken and manipulate certain aspects of you to bring out what is destructive and evil. Although justifications can alleviate feelings of guilt and shame associated with certain actions and can even deceive by giving a false sense of power and righteousness, their long-term effects are unsettling and disallowing because when you use justification, you surrender your power and shift control from yourself to others and the various situations that life may throw at you.

To live a happy and joyful life, you must take full responsibility for yourself and learn to hold yourself accountable for your actions. By doing so, you will become an empowered being who can provide whatever each situation requires and act with grace and dignity no matter what; only then will you be able to taste the true sense of your entire being and its magic!

Time

Time, is it the only valuable thing we possess in our life, or is it a collateral accumulation of existence itself? How can we make the most out of a given moment, and how can we truly understand the significance of each life period we go through?

Don't you think that some people are naturally gifted with the ability to be in the right place at the right time? They instinctively know where they should position themselves in this world, while others seem to be cursed by being always present at the wrong time. When we dig deeper into such a concept, we discover that it goes beyond analysis, emotional intelligence, or even general observations; it's a gift that extends beyond what is physical; it's a perceptional perspective of time and situations that allows the individual to have a spectacular feeling of when and where to be; this talent is closely related to one's capacity to have a tremendous sense of time.

When you examine your own life's events, themes, and deeper meanings, you'll notice that specific periods were associated with certain motifs; some were all about motion, making the most of opportunities, and reaping rewards, while others were all about paying debts, introspection, and hardcore realisations about yourself and life itself, as if each life is a resemblance of periodic changes and lessons, the problem is that many of us are unaware of such reality. As a result, we drift through life with a lack of clarity and uncertainty, which leads to never-ending misfortunes and mishaps.

You must learn how to raise your awareness level so you can understand what the present moment is about and whether you are fully present in the now. Your actions are free of any influences that may have caught on to you from past deeds and actions, or whether you are paying the debts of yesterday, whether you are free to explore the world, or there is something significant for you to understand. Such understanding will help you flow with life rather than against it, and this in itself will take you to where you need to go and present to you what you are supposed to experience; you will no longer be lost, confused, or even perplexed since you are aware of everything that was and all that is to be!

Introspection

Today, we live in a world that encourages action and all kinds of outward-directed expressions that are of tangible evidence; stillness is frequently referred to as laziness or inefficiency; the essential questions that arise are, where exactly do we fit into such an equation; are we forced to become work machines that must be relentless in their pursuit of tangible possessions? Or is this the only way to survive in this world? Both responses are somewhat correct, but the question remains: how can we adapt to such conditions and find peace and tranquillity amid such chaos?

We live with the illusion that we possess things, people, and even power, and while this may be true in the mundane realm of reality when we genuinely meditate on this idea, we discover that one's only possession is his self, which he cannot leave nor escape from. As a result, one must learn to introspect into the deepest parts of his psyche, unravelling himself into the light of truth, and only then will he be able to exist in pleasantness and peace.

You must learn to quiet the world's chaos and go on an internal journey deep within yourself because you cannot understand the world unless you first understand yourself. You are the starting point for what you call life. To indeed flow and expand your horizons, you must first master your inner world, which can only be accomplished through introspection, the process of examining your mental and emotional processes and approaching yourself in such a manner will allow you to raise your level of awareness, to the point where you are free from compulsory actions, unconscious motivations, and, most importantly, misery and pain. However, to embark on such a journey, you must first learn how to create some distance between yourself and your thoughts and emotions; only then will you be able to lose all your biases and observe them with clarity and truth.

Living in a world full of questions and secrets continually sparks our need to know and our curiosity, but you should always stay curious about yourself, for you are the beginning, the end, and everything in between!

Mirror

There is deceit in the eyes, for they steer you towards what you want to see rather than the truth. The real question is, how can one reach the point of disillusionment? How can one see the empiric truth in himself and others?

Interestingly enough, your life consists of many internal and external aspects that are mirrored by each other, your inner world creates your reality, and on the other hand, your outside world influences your internal state; it's an intricately connected web that creates what you call life, and in this understanding lies a vital realisation, that many times, what you seem to struggle with on an external level is connected to your inner self, and in a way, it's a reflection of it, for some this may appear nonsensical, or even insane; how can anything inside of me be the cause of these external problems? In fact, it is the polar opposite; these unpleasant circumstances produce my sorrow.

Internally, our motives, desires, tendencies, and habits shape the way we see the world; they formulate our likes and dislikes and what we choose to seek or avoid. These two aspects are critical because they guide us towards what we perceive to be desirable and away from what we perceive to be undesirable. These two directions shape our overall life; our desires will become a source of happiness if satisfied and a source of misery if aggrieved. While our dislikes are the things we want to get away from even though they are very much occupying us, the mirror effect manifests itself in this dynamic. For example, if you are fearful, you will find that you unconsciously guide yourself towards fear-inducing situations or even individuals; if you are hateful, you will find that you unconsciously guide yourself towards hate-evoking people, and the same thing goes for the opposite qualities, don't you see that those who are happy tend to attract to themselves even more happiness, peace, and abundance!

The point is that you can only become more of what you already are because what you are is what will direct you towards what is similar in nature in the outside world, and what you focus on in others is what you are primarily concerned with within yourself, your quality. Accepting such truth can be difficult and even painful, but it is also liberating to realise that you are the creator of either your happiness or your misery and that deep within you; you hold all the keys to your satisfaction and serenity.

Layers of Emotions

The complexity and intricacy of human emotions are fascinating, but it's often overlooked by most people. Most people can only understand the basics of I'm sad, angry, or scared; they can't go deeper within themselves to unravel the profundity and intensity of how they feel, which leads to the unconscious mind taking control of one's actions, expressions, and life direction.

Try to recollect a time when a particular person or event strongly triggered you; you've most likely distinguished your emotional reaction based on the most prominent feeling you've felt; the emotion was empowered and heightened as a result of the mental differentiation you've formed. The problem is that you've only acknowledged the first visible layer of your feelings and completely ignored the deeper layers that essentially formed and forced the emotional reaction to the surface; you've left out the key points that could potentially reveal a plethora of deep-seated motives, unfulfilled desires, and wounds that need to be addressed and healed.

You must learn to understand yourself beyond the immediate inner sensory that triggers your initial emotional reaction to the outside world and instead consciously attempt to unravel your innermost self into the light to be free of all unconscious compulsions and motives that lead to pain, hurt, and misery.

Nothing can replace a life of consciousness, and to achieve that, you must become aware of every minute aspect that makes up your individuality. The most important of these are the layers of your emotions; what is standing behind your fear, what is pushing your inner force into outward harmful expressions. These questions serve as a starting point for you to emerge from the darkness and into the light. However, you must remember that the answers may not come immediately, and they may even come disguised, but you must maintain your desire to improve yourself to enjoy a life of joy and ease!

Detachment Is Attachment

Your attachments are essentially an emotional and mental extension of yourself, which may either support your well-being or lead to your destruction. Isn't it true that you're giving away your power when you link your inner condition to exterior situations and circumstances? And, if you tried to detach yourself from everything, would it be useful, or would you end up living a life that was dull and lifeless?

When we look at our attachments as a whole, we can see that they are various aspects that support our self-identity, well-being, and internal state. The problem is that such a stance is all about division, which generally leads to limitations, judgements, and prejudice because it creates a sense of separation between oneself and the rest of the world, eventually leading to a limited perception of the world.

Detachment does not necessarily imply being aloof and detached but instead adopting a more empathetic and tolerant attitude towards everything and everyone. This will allow you to become a son of the earth rather than an individual of the world, your aspirations are no longer centred on your egoistic satisfaction but rather support the collective's growth, love becomes the lens through which you see the world, and you will no longer be shackled by any self-imposed restrictions, allowing you to move one step closer to freedom.

To become inclusive in your stance in this world, you must learn to let go of the baggage of the past; yesterday's experiences should not define how you see the world today; you should not be imprisoned by what you know but rather enriched by it; and, most importantly, when you learn to see the same qualities in everything and everyone, you will be able to liberate yourself from perceptional limitations that create the illusion of division, and you will understand the truth that you are, in fact, connected to everything and everyone!

Negative Emotions Serve a Purpose

Many people believe that the experience of negative emotions is the central issue. However, this way of thinking merely scratches the surface rather than addressing the underlying issue behind such an unpleasant human experience.

We often think of certain emotions as bad, painful, and unpleasant, and we try to get rid of them in any way we can by performing certain activities that could potentially soothe them. Once we begin to feel pleasant again, we forget the pain until something comes up and reawakens it; the problem with this scenario is that many times the emotion is thought to be the problem rather than what lies behind it, we believe that when we are angry, it is simply a temper problem, that when we are scared, it is an entirely normal reaction, and so on.

These emotions are like signals, a language that speaks to you in its own way. However, you must be receptive enough to understand this inner language and gradually learn how to decode its signs and meaning.

Emotional associations are typically formed as a result of past experiences; how you were taught to perceive the world shaped your internal emotional state, and this perception developed and expanded as you gained new experiences and increased your level of awareness. The problem is that many of us were not taught emotional intelligence, and we only learned to understand our emotions on a surface level; even though human emotions have many deep and complicated levels, this shallow knowledge led us to assume that being angry, sad, or terrified is simply wrong, rather than encouraging us to understand this inner self, its wants, desires, motives, and wounds.

You must learn to accept all of your emotions; denying them will only keep you trapped and shackled by them, limiting your ability to go on an internal journey to discover their root causes and motives. Learn to embrace your emotions in all their pain, suffering, and entirety, for only then will you regain the power to truly transform your inner self and transcend beyond the past and what it has imprinted on you.

Creating Beauty

A painter sweeps his brush across a blank canvas in an attempt to bring a scene from the realm of imagination to life; an artist creates a sound meant to hypnotise and entice the ears of those who listen; art, in all of its forms, is a device for creation, an action made for those who want to transcend beyond the mundane domain of life.

When we delve deeper into the concept of beauty, we discover that it is something that each and every one of us attempts to create and aspire to have throughout the course of our lives; we are constantly on the lookout for something visually pleasing that ignites pleasantness of emotion, and although what could be described as beautiful is very much objective, the goal remains the same. It's as if we're attempting to experience the ultimate bliss on this planet by beautifying ourselves, our surroundings, or even the environment that we live in. In a way, the ecstatic feeling of being in the presence of or even embodying beauty can soothe a part of life's suffering and transform the nature of our existence.

On an individual level, you must strive to find the beauty that exists in everything, to see yourself, others, and life itself from a unique perspective, one that admires the essence of creation, and, more importantly, you must find a space for yourself where you create something pleasing, something that ignites the power of the creator within you, and in doing so, you transcend with your existence beyond life's pain and suffering, and you overcome the fleeting nature of every moment. The possibilities are endless; just find one thing that empowers you enough to create, something that causes you to lose your sense of time and space and enter a state of complete immersion, where there is no longer a barrier between your innermost self and what you create, but rather you become an instrument that serves that creation.

Beauty is there, lying in everything that exists on this grand earth, it just requires a keen eye that sees, a quiet mind that flows, and an open heart that radiates with love, may you become the light that shines bright on everything it touches!